LORI P[...]

BOOK CLUB

Guide's Greatest

GRACE STORIES

REVIEW AND HERALD® PUBLISHING ASSOCIATION

Since 1861 | www.reviewandherald.com

Published by Review and Herald® Publishing Association, Hagerstown, MD 21741-1119

Review and Herald® titles may be purchased in bulk for educational, business, fundraising, or sales promotional use. For information, please e-mail SpecialMarkets@reviewandherald.com.

The Review and Herald® Publishing Association publishes biblically-based materials for spiritual, physical, and mental growth and Christian discipleship.

The author assumes full responsibility for the accuracy of all facts and quotations as cited in this book.

All Scripture references are from the *Holy Bible, New International Version.* Copyright © 1973, 1978, 1984, International Bible Society. Used by permission of Zondervan Bible Publishers.

This book was
Edited by Lori Peckham
Designed by Ron J. Pride
Cover art by Shane L. Johnson
Typeset: Goudy 13/16

PRINTED IN U.S.A.
12 11 10 09 08   5 4 3 2 1

Library of Congress Cataloging-in-Publication Data
Guide's greatest grace stories / Lori Peckham, editor.
    p. cm.
  1. Grace (Theology)—Juvenile literature. 2. Children—Religious life. I. Peckham, Lori.
  BT761.3.G85 2008
  242'.63--dc22

                                2008032788

ISBN 978-0-8280-2390-0

Contents

Dedication and Special Thanks   6

Introduction   7

Chapter 1: One Month, Four Days to Live   9
Elva Gardner / August 24, 1955

Chapter 2: The Day My Brother Was Hanged   12
Velva B. Holt / June 5, 1963

Chapter 3: The Horse That Cost Too Much   17
Lilith Sanford Rushing / June 10, 1964

Chapter 4: Friends at Last   24
Kay Warwick / November 9, 1966

Chapter 5: The Mystery of Brother's Ax   34
Enola Chamberlin / June 5, 1968

Chapter 6: Martha's Dream Come True   40
A. M. Bartlett / June 26, 1968

Chapter 7: The Pigeons   52
Ivy R. Doherty / October 31, 1973

Chapter 8: A Great Team   62
Everett Lee Wilhelmsen / December 11, 1974

Chapter 9: Uncle Jed's Thanksgiving Dinner   68
Marvin Moore / November 24, 1976

Chapter 10: The Best Prize   77
Louise Page Craig / November 24, 1976

Chapter 11: Springtime in the Rockies   82
Dale J. Townsend / April 13, 1977

Chapter 12: "Just Kids"   91
Mary Duplex / May 27, 1981

Chapter 13: Operation Deep Freeze   99
Daniel J. Fahrbach / March 26, 1988

Chapter 14: "I'm Going to Get You!"   106
Jane Chase / April 20, 1996

Chapter 15: House in Flames   112
Jennifer Jill Schwirzer / October 21, 2000

Chapter 16: The Cucumber Squad   117
Randy Fishell / April 13, 2002

Chapter 17: Witness in the Courtroom   123
Jeane Burgess Ewald / September 4, 2004

Chapter 18: Touched by a Christmas Toad   130
Christina Dotson / December 4, 2004

Chapter 19: A Pirate Redeemed   136
Melanie Scherencel Bockmann / March 12, 2005

Chapter 20: The Valentine Box   140
Mary Chandler / February 11, 2006

Chapter 21: The Perfect Dress   144
Joan Beck / April 21, 2007

Chapter 22: Monumental Accident   149
As told to Juliana Marin by Jorge Marin / July 28, 2007

Chapter 23: Interrupted Christmas   155
Wendy Hunt / December 22, 2007

Also by Lori Peckham:
Guide's Greatest Animal Stories
Guide's Greatest Mystery Stories
Guide's Greatest Narrow Escape Stories
Insight Presents More Unforgettable Stories
Jesus in My Shoes

To order, call **1-800-765-6955.**

Visit us at **www.reviewandherald.com** for information on other Review and Herald® Products.

A special thanks to the authors we were unable to locate. If anyone can provide knowledge of their current mailing address, please relay this information to Lori Peckham, in care of the Review and Herald® Publishing Association.

Special Thanks To . . .

The *Guide* staff—both past and present—for giving these wonderful true stories a place in their magazine.

The authors of these stories, who glimpsed God's grace and found a way to share it.

Randy Fishell, the current *Guide* editor, for suggesting titles for this volume and for modeling grace in his life.

Rachel Whitaker, *Guide's* associate editor, for her helpful recommendations and for her ready, gracious smile.

Tonya Ball, *Guide's* desktop technician, for preparing this manuscript with amazing speed and a gracious spirit.

The pioneering researchers and youth professionals of the Seventh-day Adventist Church who discovered (through studies such as Valuegenesis) and wrote about the importance, especially for young people, of experiencing grace. Among them are Roger Dudley, Steve Case, Stuart Tyner, and V. Bailey Gillespie.

My husband, Kim, and son, Reef, who share a love of good stories, and listened as I read many of these aloud, and gave their thumbs-up.

"From the fullness of his grace
we have all received one blessing after another"
(John 1:16).

Introduction

What is grace? It's getting better than you deserve.

Maybe you really ought to be punished or rejected for something you did. But you aren't. You're forgiven and welcomed. Maybe you should suffer the consequences of a bad choice. But somehow you're spared that suffering. That's grace—getting better than you deserve. Pardon. Mercy. A favor.

The ultimate grace is shown to us by Jesus. "For the wages of sin is death," says the Bible (Romans 6:23). We—each of us sinful humans—deserve to die. "But the gift of God is eternal life in Jesus Christ our Lord." That's the rest of the verse, reminding us that in God's grace, He places Jesus' perfect life over our sinful one. We can be saved and live eternally—not because we've done everything right but because we love Jesus, who did do everything right.

Jesus also showed us another part of grace—doing beautiful acts of love and kindness toward others. Putting others first. And you'll find those kinds of stories in this collection as well. You'll see amazing acts of unselfishness, forgiveness, and generosity.

As you read, you'll feel the fear followed by relief, the guilt followed by forgiveness, the suspense followed by resolution. But most of all, I hope you'll feel the grace. The grace that comes from only one source—Jesus, who showed us the meaning of the word.

—Lori Peckham

One Month, Four Days to Live

by Elva Gardner

Chang Young stood at a respectful distance behind his English master's chair in the dining room in India. Clad in a starched, spotless white butler's uniform, he stood like a soldier at attention.

Chang Young was the perfect servant. He knew when to refill the master's cup of tea, when to pass the vegetables, when to bring the evening paper, when to talk, and when to keep still. There were many other things he knew, such as which shirt the master would like laid out, just when the slippers were wanted, the temperature of the bathwater, and which guests were welcome and how to get rid of those not wanted.

He also knew how to gather news around the tea plantation and how to keep the family secrets.

Chang Young was from China, and he had held

his present job as butler and valet to the master on the Indian tea plantation for several years.

Now he stood behind his master's chair in the dining room waiting for just the right moment to speak. He had just refilled the cup of tea.

"Master." (He spoke in low tones.) "One month I go China. I train new servant for master before I go."

The master did not turn to look at Chang Young. This was their usual way of talking, with Chang Young standing behind him.

"Are you looking for a wife, Chang Young? I suppose you are lonely. But there is no need for you to go to China to get a wife. I will pay the fare of a Chinese girl to come here."

"I no get married, master. I go China stay. I teach new servant to take good care of master."

"What's the matter? Aren't you getting wages enough? I'll raise your pay. How much am I paying you now?"

"Master pay plenty now. I no want more money. I go China stay."

Now the master lost his patience. "Chang Young, you aren't going to China to stay. Do you understand? If you want more pay or more help, just say so. I don't want to hear any more of this nonsense."

Chang Young was quiet, and the master was sorry he had become angry.

"Chang Young, I was angry. Forgive me."

Chang Young was still silent.

"Chang Young, why do you want to go to China?"

"I no can say. Master will laugh at me."

"Chang Young, I promise not to laugh at you. Tell me why you must go."

"Master, I go China. I die."

The master stopped eating. "Are you ill? Why haven't you told me? You shall have the best doctors."

"I no sick, master."

"Then what is this nonsense about dying?"

"Master, one month, four days today, I die."

"How do you know you are going to die one month and four days from today?"

"Master, in my country I have brother. He have wife and children. I have no family. My brother now in prison. He sentenced to die one month, four days. In my country brother can die for brother. I go China, die for brother."

Now another servant stands behind the master's chair, fills his cup of tea, lays out the shirts, and keeps his secrets.

"Greater love hath no man than this, that a man lay down his life" (John 15:13, KJV).

A long time ago a Son said to His Father. "I go; I die for my brother." Was that brother you?

2

The Day My Brother Was Hanged

by Velva B. Holt

It was a Sunday in June. I was 8, and my brother, George, was 10. We were at Grandfather Scott's house. George and I, noticing the nice warm day, started out on an "exploring expedition." We hadn't gone far when some friends joined us, and soon there were seven of us in the expedition.

Before we had gone far, we spotted a great big white house in the middle of the road. It looked as if it was standing on stilts.

"What's a house doing in the middle of the road?" I asked George, thinking he knew everything.

"It's not doing anything—can't you see?" he answered. "Bet I can beat you there." And he started running fast, but the rest of us ran faster and caught up with him.

When we got to the house, I asked again, "What's it doing here, anyway?"

"Nothing," he said. "Just moving, that's all."

"Moving!" I gasped. "I can't see it moving. It looks like it's standing still."

"Of course it's standing still, silly. It's Sunday. If it weren't Sunday, it would be moving. See those big wheels it's on? It moves when a lot of horses pull it."

I had never seen anything like that and wished it weren't Sunday so I could see it move.

We all climbed up onto the planks the house was resting on, and then George went inside. All of us followed him because he was the oldest. Then he started making funny noises to scare us. The two smaller children got so frightened that they ran for home as fast as they could, but a girl named Emily and I stayed with the three older boys.

We followed George up a stairway that led to a lot of more rooms. Then George found a door that led to an attic. He went in and suddenly shouted, loud enough to be heard clear across the field, "Who in the world is that coming?"

I thought he was teasing as usual, but then I looked out the window and saw the same thing he did.

"It's robbers!" I screamed.

Emily and I raced down the steps faster than anyone else and got to the bottom just in time to meet the intruders face-to-face. They were masked and carrying guns. I was so scared that I began to cry, and when one of them grabbed Emily, she shrieked so loudly that he let her go.

She ran and hid inside the house, and before they could get hold of me, I shoved one of the boys out of the way, and the robber took him instead. The boy kicked and screamed and bit and managed to wriggle loose.

Just then my brother showed up. With shoulders straight and chest out, he said bravely, "If you want anybody around here, you leave these kids alone and take me."

I thought that was the noblest and bravest thing a boy could do, and I was proud that he was my brother.

Things finally quieted down, and Emily and I came out of our hiding places. The robbers were gone. But so was George.

It seems rather strange now how we got to playing again and forgot all about George and the robbers. But a little while later when I went home, my mother asked me about my brother, and I had to tell her the whole story.

Mama's mouth dropped wide open, and Grandma Scott's eyes got wider and wider. Even Grandpa and Papa seemed excited. They left at once to look for George. It was getting dark, and when Grandpa returned with no signs of my brother, we were all about frantic.

I felt terribly guilty for not coming right home to let them know, and even more so when Grandma and Mama got to telling all the terrible things that might be happening to George. We had not heard much about kidnapping in those days, or we would have called the police immediately.

Papa said, "There's only one place we didn't look, and that was in the Shermans' barn. I'm going to look there right now."

It was a good thing he thought of that, because as he was climbing up the steps to the haymow, he heard voices that sounded as if they were speaking in a foreign language. He was suspicious at once, so he sneaked up to the top step of the ladder to listen more closely. And there was George—gagged and bound, hanging head down from one of the rafters!

Papa didn't waste a minute's time getting up in that haymow. Then he began speaking in a language everyone understood! He really talked in plain words, for the "robbers" were just teenage boys who had put on masks and armed themselves with toy rifles. They had managed to get George tied up by the feet and were ready to leave him hanging there.

Papa threatened to call the police. Then those great big boys started blubbering like babies. Tears ran down their cheeks, and they begged him not to.

He asked them why they had done such an awful thing, and they said, "We saw it done in the movies and wanted to try it out ourselves. It looked like fun, but I guess it isn't so much fun when you get caught." They promised never to do anything like it again.

In spite of all the bravery those big boys had shown earlier in the day, they turned out to be sniveling crybabies. And I still think that George was the bravest of all. He hadn't been to the movies to learn how to be brave. He had just tried to save us other children from being hurt.

3

The Horse
That Cost Too Much

by Lilith Sanford Rushing

Every morning when Carl woke up he'd run to the window and gaze at his horse in the nearby pasture.

This morning his sister, Paula, scolded him. "You worship that horse, Carl! And you paid too much for him, too!"

"I wish you'd stop talking that way!" Carl countered. "He's my horse—I worked for him."

Carl left the window and ran ahead of his sister down the stairs. Grandma was putting breakfast on the table. For four weeks now Mom and Dad had been away on a business trip.

When Grandma went to the stove for something, Paula whispered to Carl, "What would Mom and Dad say if they knew how you made the money for your horse?"

Carl looked away from her. He did wish it hadn't been that way. It all came back to him as he ate his breakfast.

As long as he could remember, he'd longed for a horse. The family lived a mile from town and had a 20-acre farm—such a nice home for a horse! Last spring on the Browns' farm there had been a young horse for sale, but Carl hadn't had enough money saved to buy it. His father had thought Carl should pay for the horse himself.

"It will teach you the value of money," Dad had said.

Carl had begun saving at once, and many times he and Paula had walked to the Browns' farm to look at the horse. Carl even named it before he got it— Prince.

A week after their parents went away, Mr. Brown had stopped at the Staley home. He had startling news. "Some people want to buy Prince today. And," he added, "they have the money."

Carl had felt stricken. He couldn't lose Prince! "Mr. Brown," he had said, "just give me two weeks, will you, please? I have half the money now. I'll get the other half as soon as I can."

But Mr. Brown had said he had to have all the money that very minute. Paula had run to collect all the money she'd saved, and Carl had run into the house, wondering what he could do. He had seen

Grandma's purse hanging on the wall. She'd gone to the henhouse for eggs. Quickly Carl had grabbed the purse and taken all the money that was in it. Now he had enough!

He paid for the horse, and Mr. Brown had turned Prince over to him. But what a tangle he'd made for himself, for he knew that any day Grandma would discover her money was gone. So Carl had started to work several hours a day for Mr. Gibson in his grocery store. And this was where the second problem came in: Mr. Gibson insisted that Carl work on Sabbath mornings. For three weeks Grandma had thought Carl had gone to Sabbath school and church, but instead he'd been working at the grocery store. He hadn't paid tithe on what he'd earned, either. When his weekly allowance had come from his parents, he had used it to put the money back in Grandma's purse. Last week he'd replaced all he owed Grandma, and he'd quit his job at the grocery store. But a heavy feeling of guilt lay on his heart. Paula was always scolding him about his misdeeds, and any day his parents would be coming back.

After breakfast Carl went to work mowing the lawn and trimming the shrubbery. Surely, he reasoned, he could make up for the tithe he had failed to pay, and in time he could pay Paula for her share in the purchase price. But he could never get back the precious hours he'd missed from church while he had worked. And how could he blot out the memory of working on those Sabbath mornings?

Two days later his parents returned, and the next day Carl and Paula's aunt and cousins came from the East. What a wonderful time the children had! They held big watermelon feasts on the front lawn. Paula and Carl and their cousins—two boys and a girl—explored every foot of the small farm. They waded in the creek and climbed trees. But the best fun of all was riding Prince. It seemed as if Prince loved the children as much as they loved him! If one of them fell off, the horse would stop and wait until they got back on. Still, Carl could not forget how he had paid for Prince.

The week passed quickly, and it was almost time for the cousins to leave. Mother suggested they go to the park near town for one last picnic. At once many voices arose.

"I'm going to ride Prince!"

"No, I am!"

"I am!"

Mother said that the children could take turns. They would have to ride on the grassy slope at the side of the highway.

After the picnic Mother drove the Staleys' car back to the farm, and Aunt Georgia drove hers, going along slowly while the children took turns riding Prince.

They were halfway home, and Paula was on Prince's back. Without any warning something strange and terrifying happened.

The grass on both sides of the highway had grown tall. Paula was a good rider, but suddenly Prince sank down into the earth so that only his neck and head could be seen! Paula was thrown over Prince's head and off to one side, looking like a rag doll tossed carelessly in the grass. Mother and Aunt Georgia stopped their cars at once, and everybody got out, shouting and talking at the same time.

Paula got up, unhurt. But Prince seemed to be stuck in a hole that the tall grass had hidden. His head and neck were thrust out at an unnatural angle.

Mother said, "Oh, dear, what has happened to Prince? We can thank God that Paula is safe, but the horse! His legs may be broken!"

"He's in a deep hole," Aunt Georgia wailed. "Can't somebody help us?"

The children stood about with sad faces, but Carl's was the most tragic.

Cars going along the highway began stopping. Help would be brought from town. Mr. Staley would be summoned. Equipment from the road construction crew would have to come and pull the horse out.

"But you can't pull a horse out of a hole like that without badly injuring or killing him," someone said.

Carl heard everything. And every word cut deep

gashes in his heart. Some of the men found out what was holding Prince so tight. The horse had fallen through some steel grates that led to an underground culvert. The hazardous drain had been hidden by the tall grass. Nobody knew what to do. It would take an acetylene torch to burn the rods away, a man said. And that would scare the horse out of his wits, he added. More and more people stopped by, but no one seemed to have a solution.

Carl, standing apart from the others, saw the anguished look in Prince's eyes. They seemed to ask, "Why does this horrible thing hold me?"

Now Carl heard someone say, "It may be that the horse is injured so badly that he'll just have to be shot where he is."

Carl covered his face with his hands and sank down in the tall grass. "Dear God, please don't let Prince die," he prayed. Never had Carl prayed so earnestly.

Suddenly the crowd hushed. They were seeing a miracle. Prince's body began to rise from the grating, higher and higher! Suddenly he gave one mighty lunge—and was out! Carl was so amazed that he could hardly breathe. Prince was out of the terrible drain! His left side was skinned, and his gray coat was dark with sweat, but he was out. Prince turned to Carl and walked toward him.

"Thank You, God! Thank You!" was all the boy

could say. "Even though I failed You, You heard my prayer!" Carl sensed that he'd just discovered something about a thing called grace.

That very evening Carl told his parents about how he had gotten the money to pay for Prince. He said, "Dad, I need to sell Prince. I want to pay for my—for what I've done."

Father said, "We'll have to think this over."

Carl slept little that night. The next morning he didn't run to the window to see Prince. He dressed and slowly descended the stairs.

Father said, "Carl, I've sold Prince for you. He isn't your horse now. Here's the money. You can pay back your sister what she lent you, and you can catch up on the tithe you owe."

Carl's head dropped. Sadly he asked, "Who bought Prince? Will they be good to him?"

"Yes, the owner will be good to him," Father said. "You see," he said with a smile, "we sold him to your sister, Paula. Maybe someday you can buy another horse for yourself."

"Oh, Dad!" he beamed. "I'm glad—I'm so glad Prince won't be leaving his pasture. And I promise I'll never work on Sabbath again." He ran and put both arms around his father's neck.

4

Friends at Last

by Kay Warwick

Hank was so mad that he could hardly see straight. What was Tobe Turner up to, sneaking into Sand Cave that way? He knew that Tobe had been ordered to stay out of the cave, so he must be up to some mischief.

Hank watched the entrance of the cave for a minute; he was pretty sure that Tobe hadn't seen him. Then he wheeled his bicycle around and headed for Perkins' store as fast as he could pedal.

The combination country store and gas station sat on a corner of a quiet, neglected crossroads, but it did have a telephone. Hank was relieved when his friend's drawling voice came over the wire.

"What's up, Hank? Sounds like you're in a tizzy." That was Bill Todd, never in a hurry. But he must hurry this time!

Hank quickly explained about seeing Tobe. Then he added, "Don't forget a thing. Extra candles and our rope and jackets, and both flashlights. We're going to find out what Tobe's up to!"

"He's probably goin' to steal some specimens to sell to the souvenir shop over at Big Cave," Bill said slowly. "Well, hang up, Hank. I'm on my way. Meet you at the cave entrance."

All the way back to the cave Hank's thoughts whirled as fast as his bicycle wheels. In the past he'd tried often enough, he thought, *really tried* to make a friend out of Tobe. He'd even asked him to church. But he'd finally given up. Some people you just couldn't help. And then when Tobe Turner and his gang had laid for them after Young People's Meeting—well, that had finished Hank and the other fellows, too.

It's no wonder the Reeses and Turners have always been bitter enemies, especially if all the Turners have been like Tobe, Hank thought resentfully. He'd always known of the rivalry between the two families. It went back all the way to the Civil War when the Reeses belonged to the Kentucky Cavalry and the Turners belonged to the Home Guard. Kentucky had been mostly on the side of the North, but many of its people had fought for the South.

Hank and Bill belonged to a spelunking club and were proud to be cavers. They had explored Sand

Cave many times and never destroyed any of its natural beauties. But Tobe Turner and his friends had gone into the cave at different times. They'd taken specimens and littered the tunnels so that Mr. Randall, who owned the land the cave was on, had told Tobe never to go in the cave again.

Hank parked his bike at the cave's entrance, a gaping maw beneath a limestone ledge. He studied the tracks in the soft sand and was pretty sure that Tobe was still in there. Well, they would find out what he was up to and catch him at it! They owed him something anyway for the dirty tricks he'd so often played on them.

Bill was panting heavily when he finally bicycled up the hill to the opening. The basket on his bicycle was full of the things the boys always carried when they went into any cave.

"Hurry up, Bill," Hank hissed. "He's still in there, and I think he's alone. I didn't see anyone else go in with him."

"OK, OK. Let's check everything first." Bill portioned out the candles, flashlights, and jackets, and slung their nylon rope over his shoulder.

The two young men advanced carefully. Once inside, they flashed their lights downward, watching for Tobe's tracks in the sand. There would be only one way for them to go for a while, through the main tunnel.

"This jacket sure feels good," Hank whispered.

"Yeah," Bill answered. "It's only 56 degrees in here, winter and summer." Then he exclaimed, "Oh, that—that rat! Look what he's doing. He's chipping samples of gypsum—" His words trailed off in disgust.

"Up to his old tricks—he's a thief and a sneak!" Hank muttered. "Everyone knows we're only allowed to take pictures, never destroy the natural growths."

After they'd been walking quite a while, Bill said, "This is as far as I've ever been."

They had reached a place where the tunnel became considerably narrower, and they had to stoop sometimes to keep from banging their heads.

Hank knelt down and studied the floor. The sand had disappeared, and the surface was hard. He couldn't make out any footprints.

"I've been down this passage once, and it ends in a stream," he said slowly.

Bill was carefully studying a low, horizontal fissure at floor level in the side of the tunnel. "This is only a crawlway, but it looks as if someone's moved this rubble around a bit. Maybe Tobe. Here's a large boulder that might have been pushed to one side."

"We'll try this way." Suppressed excitement made Hank's voice unsteady. Exploring a new place in a cave was always challenging.

The boys crawled into the narrow opening.

"If we were any larger, this sure would be a tight

squeeze," Bill complained as he wriggled along on his stomach.

"Be quiet and crawl," Hank ordered as he pushed himself along.

The floor was solid travertine, and the roof was so low that Hank couldn't raise himself on his elbows without bumping his head. The tight passageway sloped gently downward, then curved to the right. Soon the boys squirmed through an opening into a larger tunnel. Bill flopped over onto his back, sighing in exhaustion.

"Aw, come on," Hank urged. "We can walk now."

The boys kept their voices down, pausing occasionally to listen, hoping to hear Tobe's chipping hammer. They were descending all the time, and now the floor of the cave was damp under their feet.

Suddenly Hank stopped and held up his hand. "Listen!"

He swiveled around just in time to see two small pebbles come slithering, rolling, bounding down the incline. The sound of raucous, hooting laughter echoed through the tunnel. Then dead silence.

Bill didn't need to be told what had happened. He turned, and the boys ran back to the tight passageway. Hank crawled into it first. One behind the other they wriggled through as fast as they could. However, when Hank reached the end of the crawlway, his worst fears were realized.

He lay there panting, suddenly warm in the cool-
ness of the cave.

"Well, go on," Bill said impatiently from behind
him.

"We can't." Hank's voice was dull, flat. "The entrance is blocked, probably by that boulder we saw.
Our friend Tobe . . . " He swallowed and took a deep
breath. "Our friend has walled us in here. We're
trapped!"

Bill was silent. "Well, it's the other way out for
us," he said calmly. "Come on."

Hank almost asked, "What if there's no other way
out?" but he bit his tongue and followed his friend.

They both felt a little better when they reached
the larger passage and could stand up.

"Well, mean as Tobe Turner is, I never thought
he'd do a thing like that," Bill remarked.

Hank said slowly, "I don't believe he would let
us—die—in here. He might come back and move
that rock later on. He probably just wanted to give us
a good scare."

"Well, he's succeeded, as far as I'm concerned,"
Bill said.

The passageway curving ahead seemed endless,
but they noticed their feet getting wetter, and they
were extra careful not to slip. And then they were
able to hear water running.

"The stream!" Hank cried, and stepped up his

pace. "Probably this joins the main tunnel and goes beside the underground river."

After several more curves, the boys saw that Hank's guess was right. They entered another tunnel, and ahead of them the water sounded louder than ever.

"There's a light!" Bill said.

The boys broke into a careful run, and Hank yelled, "Hey, Tobe, we've got you now!" as he recognized the figure ahead of them.

Hank thought exultantly, *So the passage does join the original one*. He hurried after the other boy. Tobe heard them, turned, and looked at them briefly, then began to run. His light wavered and flickered on the rock walls.

"Careful! Don't slip," Bill warned, and Hank slowed down. But not the youth they were chasing. He ran faster, turned a corner, and was out of their sight.

Then a scream split the silence of the cave, and the boys rounded the corner. All they saw ahead of them were the rushing waters of the underground stream. Tobe Turner had disappeared!

They skidded to a stop. Bill yelled, "There he is!"

Tobe was in the water. As his head broke the surface, he screamed again, then was swept away by the current.

Hank would have prayed for help if he'd had time,

but then perhaps his whole being was one large prayer. He knew only that they needed help—lots of it if they were to rescue the drowning boy.

He ran along the bank of the stream for a short distance. Then the passageway widened into a large room, and the stream made its way across the far side of it. Hank hesitated for a moment.

Then Bill was at his side, the coil of rope in his hand. "Cut across! We can beat Tobe to the bend!"

One glance showed Hank the wisdom of Bill's suggestion. The two boys streaked across the cave's uneven floor, hoping to reach the curve of the river on the farther side before the current carried Tobe there.

At the end of the stream Hank stopped, and the boys worked quickly with the rope. They tied one end of it around Hank's waist. (He'd muttered, "I'm the best swimmer," and Bill didn't argue.) They snagged the rope around a jutting rock; and then Bill wound the other end about his waist and braced himself.

They were not a moment too soon. At first Hank thought Tobe had been swept on past their vantage point, but then he saw the boy surface a few feet from them, his arms flailing, his face greenish-white in the glare of Bill's flashlight.

Hank plunged into the water. It was deep and icy cold, and he couldn't touch bottom. The stream was about eight feet wide at the bend. He swam strongly, praying that he could reach Tobe. Once he grabbed for Tobe and missed. Then he forced himself forward desperately in a mighty lunge and caught Tobe by the arm.

Tobe fought him. By this time he had lost all reason and all sense of direction, and Hank thought that surely Tobe would be torn from his grasp. But Hank hung on, and then he felt the grip of the rope tighten about his waist, and he knew that Bill was pulling them to the bank.

Hank lay panting on the hard rock floor while Bill systematically worked over Tobe until he gasped and spluttered. Then all three of them lay exhausted, breathing deeply as they tried to recover.

When Tobe could finally speak, his first words were "I—I don't know what to say." His face was shamed, and he couldn't look straight at them. He stammered, "I—I really wasn't trying to kill you. I knew you could get out this end of the tunnel. I just wanted to scare you when I blocked it."

He raised his face and looked directly into Hank's eyes. "After all I've done to you, after the way your folks and mine have always hated one another, why would you come after me? Why should you risk your life to save mine?"

Hank hesitated. There was only one answer to that question, but before he could say it, Tobe said it for him. "Because you're a Christian—is that it?"

Hank nodded. "I couldn't do anything else."

Tobe was quiet for several minutes, and neither Hank nor Bill spoke. Hank somehow sensed that Tobe was taking a good look at himself and at them and seeing things differently than he had ever seen them before.

Tobe Turner got to his feet, stumbled over to where Hank was sitting, and held out his hand. "Put it there," he said gruffly. "All I can say—is—thanks. Things are sure going to be a lot different with me from now on."

For the first time in a hundred years a Reese and a Turner clasped hands in friendship.

5

The Mystery of Brother's Ax

by Enola Chamberlin

One summer when I was in my early teens, I visited an aunt who lived in a small town. At church I saw an older man who looked interesting, and asked my aunt who he was. She said he was the most devout person she had ever known.

"But they tell he hasn't always been good," she explained. "When he was young, he didn't even believe in God. He was pretty wild, I guess. Then something happened, and he changed overnight."

"What happened?" I asked.

My aunt said she didn't know—and she didn't know anyone else who did.

"Well," I said, "I'm going to find out!"

So the next day, with the warm breeze smelling of ripening fruit, I set out to this man's house to ask him. Probably if I had been older or younger, I would have turned back after I started. But I remembered that he was such a kind-looking man, and I didn't even consider that he might not be willing to answer my questions.

I found him sitting, as he often did, on the front porch of the small house in which he lived alone. He had an open Bible on his knees.

He said hello and smiled with his clear blue eyes as well as with his lips. I introduced myself and told him that I was a visitor in town. Then, because I was finally a bit embarrassed about my errand, my voice cracked. "They tell me," I began, "that you used to not believe in God and that you changed overnight, it seems. No one knows why. Is it a secret?"

The smile did not leave his face, which relieved me! He motioned me to a chair. I sat down timidly.

"No, it's not a secret," he said. "It's just that it has been several years since anyone has had the interest or the"—he paused and looked like a boy up to mischief—"gall, courage, effrontery—whatever you like to call it—to ask me."

I smiled back at him. My timidity, my embarrassment, were gone. He had made me feel as though I had known him all my life.

"Well, I'm asking," I said, copying his mischievous manner.

"So I'll tell you," he said. "But it goes back quite

a piece of time, and I may be slow. But if you'll put up with me, I'd love to talk about it."

"And I'd love to hear you talk," I said and made sure I looked ready to listen.

He said, "If people told you that once I didn't believe in God, they probably told you also that I didn't amount to much by the time I'd grown up. That wasn't the fault of my folks," he hastened to inform me. "They were as good as any folks could be. I just didn't follow where they led."

"But you're following them now," I said.

"Yes, thank God," he said. "It was when I was about 25. We lived in the Midwest then. My mother, God bless her, was, as so many mothers are, partial to the child who caused her the most trouble. In our family I was that child. When I wrote that I was coming home, she remembered how I liked chicken and dumplings, and she went out and bought a hen, planning to cook it when I got there. It had to be a live hen because we couldn't buy chickens ready for the pot as you can now."

He stopped. Slowly he turned the leaves of his Bible. It seemed as if he was looking back, trying to get his story just right.

"I had a sister 10 years old," he continued. "She was a funny little tyke, always making friends with animals. She had a tame crow at one time. At another time she had a lizard that would crawl up to her neck and lie with its head in her hair as she played. Well, when this hen came on the premises, she immediately began to make a pet of it. I should have known this would happen, but I didn't think about it."

He was silent again. I feared to speak lest I sidetrack him.

"Mother knew in a way," he went on, "but she was a practical woman. She had bought that hen to make a dumpling dinner, and she never saw the bird in any other light."

He drew a long breath. "I can realize now the anguish my sister suffered when she heard that the hen was to be killed. Being the withdrawn type she was, she didn't say a word to anyone. She greeted me warmly when I came home in the evening, but I don't think she slept a bit that night. From my bed I could hear her turning and tossing on hers. Once she got up and went outdoors. I learned later that she was telling her pet goodbye."

He turned his pleasant, wrinkled face toward mine. "Don't ever take anything or anyone for granted," he said slowly. "Ask God to help you find what is underneath the way people act."

He turned his eyes from me and looked out to where the heat dazzled on the street. "Morning came and breakfast," he went on. "Mother told me to get the chicken and cut off its head so she could dress it and have it cool before she cooked it. As I picked up the hen, I marveled at how tame she was, but she did squawk her indignation as I carried her by her legs to the chopping block."

He paused and swallowed hard, as if the next part was difficult to say. "I laid her head down on the block and picked up the ax. I raised it high, aimed it at her neck, and began to bring it down with great force. Then there came a scream and the flurry of a dress—and my sister threw herself over that hen and right under the falling ax."

I shuddered.

"I had no time to think, no time to do anything." He was almost whispering now. "No earthly force could have kept that sharp blade from striking down and cutting my sister in two. But the ax never came down."

He stopped and held the Bible close in his wrinkled hands. "In that instant," he went on, "I know that God gave me the power to control that ax, to hurl it forcibly backward, where it fell harmlessly to the ground. In that instant I knew that there was a God and that He had saved both my sister and me. And so I changed—not overnight. I changed much quicker than that—in a moment's time."

Tears stood in my eyes. He saw them.

"Yes," he said, "it makes you want to cry. And that is what I did when I dropped down and took my sobbing sister in my arms." He smiled lightly. "And that fool hen," he said, "she stood there and clucked and picked at the tears on our faces."

I heaved a deep sigh. "And so you didn't kill the chicken after all," I said.

"Kill her!" he cried out. "I'd have gone hungry all my days rather than have killed or eaten that chicken. We had macaroni and cheese for dinner." He smiled brightly now. "I still remember how good it tasted."

I thanked him for telling me and went away marveling at the ways in which God shows His grace to us humans.

6

Martha's Dream Come True

by A. M. Bartlett

The meeting had lasted a little longer than usual, and Martha was hurrying home. She knew that her mother would be worried about her and that her father would probably be quite angry. Hers was a strict family, and Martha, together with her older brother and younger sister, was not allowed to be out on the street after nine o'clock in the evening.

For several weeks Martha had been attending a series of meetings in the beautiful new Adventist church in the Sario district of the city of Manado. At first she had tried to get her parents interested in the meetings, but they had only ridiculed her, so lately she had not said anything. Tonight, however, it was nearly 10:00 p.m., and her father was sure to investigate where she had been. The meeting had gone on later than usual because the young evangelist had made an appeal to all who wished to be loyal to God to come forward. Martha had gone forward, and in the meeting afterward she had decided to join the baptismal class that was formed. The baptism was set to take place in two weeks.

As Martha walked along the darkened street, she knew she had done the right thing. She also knew her parents would not approve. She had hoped they wouldn't know about her determination until after the baptism, because then it would be too late to stop her. But she knew she could not hide it now, and she prayed for strength as she approached the house.

"Martha, where have you been? We have been worried about you," said her mother when Martha entered the front door.

"I'm so sorry, Mother. I just couldn't come any sooner," said the girl as she quietly tried to slip into the room where she slept with her sister. She knew it wouldn't help any to discuss the matter.

"You didn't answer your mother's question," her father said sternly. "Where have you been, Martha?"

Martha answered bravely. "I've been at the evangelistic meeting, Father. It lasted longer than usual this evening. That's why I was late getting home."

"What! Are you still attending those silly Adventist meetings? I thought I told you several weeks ago to give up that foolishness."

"Yes, Father." The evenness of her voice surprised even Martha. "I have been going every night, and I don't find the study of God's Word either silly or foolish."

"Now, don't get impudent, young lady," snapped Father. "I suppose the next thing you will tell us is that you want to leave your parents' church and join the Adventists."

"Yes," Martha said. "That's right. I have already joined the baptismal class. There will be a baptism two weeks from now, and I am planning to join the Adventist Church at that time." Again Martha was surprised at her calmness. It seemed almost as though someone else had spoken the words.

The scene that followed was not pleasant. Mother cried, and Father shouted. The other members of the family also joined in with cutting remarks. In the end, Martha was weeping as her father made it clear that she had attended her last Adventist meeting. As for baptism, it was unthinkable. If she should ever be baptized, she would be immediately turned out of the house and disowned.

The next few days were very difficult for Martha. Home had always been a pleasant place, and although there was stern discipline, there was also love and a feeling of peace. Now that feeling was gone, and she seemed to be a prisoner. She was constantly watched so as not to be able to visit any of the

Adventists; and, of course, there was no chance to go to the evening meetings.

Then one afternoon her parents were unexpectedly called away, and her brother and sister drifted away on errands of their own. When it was time to go to the meeting, Martha was alone. Quickly she changed her dress and slipped out to the church where the meetings were being held. During the song service she found Mrs. Lie, and through her tears told her of all that had happened. When the sad story was finished, Martha added, "But I will be baptized with the rest. I know the Lord will open the way. And please, Mrs. Lie, please pray for my father, too."

Her parents were already at home when Martha came in. Again many harsh things were said, and Father gave her a severe whipping. The days dragged by, and Martha was seldom out of sight of some member of the family. Only once more did she get a chance to attend one of the meetings, and, of course, she was again severely punished when she came home.

Many times Martha longed for the peace and joy that used to fill her home. During the long nights, when she felt the most lonely, Satan seemed to accuse her, telling her that all would be happy again if she would only give up these ideas of the Adventists and go again to the church her parents belonged to. All she could do was pray, and many times every day she prayed for strength to be true to Jesus and to be obedient to His will.

Then a strange new idea came, and Martha dreamed of a home that was happy again. But this was not a home like it used to be—it was an infinitely happier place, where Mother and Father studied the Bible and where the whole family went to the Adventist Church together every Sabbath morning. Just to imagine such a thing made her feel warm and happy, and Martha found herself praying about it more and more. At night she frequently dreamed about it, and during the day it was always in her thoughts. Could such a thing ever be?

The day of the baptism finally came. Martha had prayed again and again that the Lord would work it out some way so she could attend the meeting and be baptized, but she knew there was little hope. Several times during those two weeks her father had mentioned this day with bitter threats, and Mother had also warned her of the results if she should insist on going ahead with her plans for baptism.

At the breakfast table she expected her parents to repeat their threats, but nothing was said. It seemed as though they had entirely forgotten. For several days she had not been permitted to leave the house alone, and so she was even more surprised when, after the dishes were washed and the morning chores were finished, each member of the family drifted off.

Martha suddenly realized that she was left alone. As she looked at the clock, her heart almost skipped a beat. There was still plenty of time to get dressed and walk to the church before the baptismal service began.

Hastily Martha dressed, then carefully folded a change of clothing in a clean towel. She hurried to the church, fearing every moment that someone would try to stop her. Not until she was seated and, she hoped, quite lost in the large congregation did she begin to breathe easily. Then a new fear came into her heart: *I haven't been attending the baptismal classes. Maybe the pastor will not allow me to be baptized.* The girl almost cried at the thought, and suddenly she wished she had not come. Then she heard her name softly spoken, and a warm hand clasped her own as Mrs. Lie slipped into the seat beside her.

"Ah, Martha, we are so glad to see you. We have been praying for you so often. It looks as though God has answered our prayers, for I see you are prepared for the baptism." Mrs. Lie's words were soft, but her eyes were bright, and her smile was genuine.

Tearfully Martha told her all that had happened, and then they went together to talk with Pastor Lie. He was also very happy to see Martha, and after asking a few pointed questions about her love for the Savior and her determination to be loyal to Him, he told her to sit with the other candidates.

Her joy was full, and it proved to be a perfect day. After a stirring sermon by a visiting pastor from the union mission headquarters, 34 people were baptized. After this wonderful experience these new members partook of their first Communion service in the Seventh-day Adventist Church.

All of these things had taken quite a long time, and it was already long past dinnertime when Martha left the church and headed for home with a happy song in her heart.

Her happy, almost heavenly, feelings, however, were rudely snatched from her when Martha entered the house. Angrily her father demanded to know where she had been. After Martha admitted having been baptized, he seized a piece of rattan and beat her, almost to unconsciousness. When he stopped striking her, he demanded of each of the other members of the family why they had not prevented her from going to the church. Finally all of them, including the father, admitted that they had entirely forgotten about Martha that morning. Bruised and bleeding, Martha knew why they had forgotten. She knew this was God's plan, and even in her pain she was happy.

The following morning there was nothing but bitterness. Father announced that Martha would have to leave home. He would give her until noon, he said, to find another place to stay, and she would never again be considered a member of the family. Mother burst into tears, and Martha was heartbroken, but she knew Father would not change his mind. All morning she was sick from the things she had suffered, but no one offered to help her. She was ignored, and the other members of the family seldom spoke to her.

At noon she took her little bundle of clothes and left the house. She was only 16 years old and didn't know where to go. She thought of going to see Pastor Lie, but she knew that no matter how kind he and his wife were, they had no place for her. Slowly she made her way along the street. Her body was bruised, and her heart was almost breaking.

The only relative who lived near was her grandmother, and she decided to go there first. If Grandmother should refuse to accept her, then she would have to try to seek a home among her new Adventist friends.

"Come in, child," said the old woman in response to Martha's knock. When they were seated inside, she continued, "I've been expecting you, because I know you have no place else to go. The Adventists"—and she spoke with disgust—"wouldn't dare to take you in, for your father would make trouble aplenty for them if they did."

Martha knew she wasn't welcome here, either. She let her head fall into her hands and cried. The whole world seemed to be against her. She had been so happy yesterday and so sure that Jesus had opened the door and that it was His will for her to be baptized. As she sat here now, she wasn't so sure. If the Lord really loved her, why did He let things happen like this?

"Crying won't help," said Grandmother sternly. "Your father is right, of course. It is very foolish of you to go and join the Adventist Church. But I think you will come to your senses soon enough. You can stay with me on condition that you never go to church on Saturday or attend any Adventist meetings at other times. Is that clear?"

Martha nodded, but in her heart she was counting the days until Sabbath. Somehow, she would have to find another place to stay before then.

The afternoon seemed endless, and when she went to bed that night, Martha could only cry softly into her pillow. She tried to dream those happy thoughts again, about her whole family going to church together on Sabbath and all being peaceful and even happier than it used to be. But it was hard. Everything seemed so dark. It seemed that her dream could never come true.

Two days went by, and Martha heard nothing of home. She tried to fit into the new pattern of things and act cheerful, but her heart was as heavy as lead. Grandmother seldom even spoke to her, and the girl knew she was not welcome. It seemed so hopeless.

She must find some other place to stay soon, for she was determined to go to church on Sabbath. But where could she go?

"Is Martha here?" She heard a familiar voice as she was washing some clothes in the backyard. She recognized it at once as her father's voice, but it sounded strangely different. She was both thrilled and frightened. Why had he come now?

"Here I am, Father," she called, trying to keep her voice under control.

A moment later he strode around the house, and Martha stood up to meet him. Their eyes met, and for a long moment neither spoke. As she searched his face, she knew that something had happened, and her mind raced. Was Mother sick? Had there been some terrible accident? If only he would say something!

"It's all right now, Martha." Father's voice was shaky and husky. "You can come home again."

Martha wanted to shout or cry, and a thousand questions came flooding into her mind at once. She opened her mouth to speak, but Father stopped her with his hand. "Get your things, dear. I'll tell you all about it on the way home."

Breathlessly she waited for Father to speak after they left the house, but they walked along in silence for several minutes. Finally he began to talk, his voice subdued.

"I felt terrible the day I sent you away, Martha. I

couldn't do any work at all. That night all I could think about was your shocked expression when I told you to go. And I was so sorry that I had beaten you so harshly. Please forgive me. I sincerely believed, though, that I was in the right and that I was punishing you for your own good. You've got to believe me, Martha, and forgive me."

Her throat grew so tight that it hurt as Father was speaking. She wanted to throw her arms around his neck and kiss him and tell him that it was all past and forgotten, but the lump in her throat wouldn't let her make a sound.

Father went on with his story. "That night I rolled and tossed and couldn't sleep for a long time. When I finally did go to sleep, I had a terrible dream. Everything was dark, and it seemed that something dreadful was about to happen. Then I saw a cross in the sky, and it had bright beams of light shining from it that hurt my eyes. I was afraid, and then I heard a voice speaking directly to me. It said, 'You have been fighting against God.' Then the cross vanished, and it was even darker than it had been before. I woke up in a cold sweat and couldn't go back to sleep again. The voice kept ringing in my ears: 'You have been fighting against God.' The next day I determined to go to the meeting and hear Pastor Lie. Could it be that he was really preaching the truth? If so, I knew I really had been fighting against God.

"That night I went to the meeting. I expected to see you there, but you didn't come. I brought my Bible, and as the evangelist preached, I looked up every text he used. Long before the sermon was over, I was convinced that he was indeed preaching the truth and that you have *not* been following cunningly devised fables. At the end Pastor Lie made a call, and I went forward, Martha. I have already talked it over with Mother, and we want to be baptized too and join the Adventist Church with you."

By this time Martha was crying again, but now they were tears of joy. Her dream was coming true. Right when she had been the most discouraged and it was the hardest to believe in the dream, God had given another dream to her father.

The next Sabbath not only Martha but the whole family went to church, and a few weeks later her parents and her brother and sister were baptized. Everything turned out even better than Martha's dream!

7

The Pigeons

by Ivy R. Doherty

"Guess what, Mom?" I said, replacing the telephone receiver in its cradle. "All the Durands are sick—Timbuktu flu, by the sound of Mrs. Durand's voice."

"Oh," Mom said softly. "I wondered why things were so quiet over there." She shifted her attention briefly from the hot cereal she'd been stirring to say, "We'll have to see what we can do to help."

"I'll take care of Mr. Durand's pigeons," I announced.

Mom gave a fleeting smile. "You and those pigeons," she said.

"Aw, Mom, you know I'd look after them even if I didn't like them," I protested. "Mr. Durand is so great that I'd do anything for him. And besides, someone will have to check on those three nests with eggs that will hatch any time now."

"Hustle with your breakfast, then, Marty," said Mom, "so you can check on the birds on your way to school. I'll see to the ailing humans."

That's Mom stated in one phrase. She's always seeing to ailing humans. Some ail in spirit, some in mind, and some in body. Mom lives by the text on the plaque over her sink: "Thou shalt love the Lord thy God with all thy heart, and . . . thy neighbor as thyself" (Matt. 22:37-39, KJV). But I think Mom loves her neighbors more than herself.

Outdoors, the air was sharp with spring frost, and that made me want to let off energy, so I started bellowing, "Oh, what a beautiful morning! Oh, what a beautiful day . . ."

Mr. Warriner's full-moon head came up over the hedge. "Beautiful morning, my eye!" he snarled.

I shut up mousetrap quick, especially when I saw Aristotle, his German shepherd, peering through the bushes at me.

We have variety in next-door neighbors, I thought as I climbed the ladder to the pigeon's loft. *Mr. Durand is good and kind; Mr. Warriner is grouchy to the point of being hateful. I guess I should be used to him after two years, but I'm not. Mom and Dad say there must be some reason for his bad attitude and we must try to understand him.*

The pigeons hopped around all bright-eyed and excited, which was a nice change after the way Mr.

Warriner had acted. The two peepers that had hatched a week before wobbled their knobby heads about, and their mouths gaped for a handout. They were so ugly that it was hard to imagine them growing into sleek-feathered beauties, and I thought, *Only a mother could love kids that look like you!*

I dipped the metal scoop into the mixture of wheat, peas, beans, and corn and enjoyed its smell as I fed the pigeons. They ate greedily. I gave them drinking water, filled their baths, and cleaned their nests. Then I took a minute to stroke the blue-check beauty in nest three, my favorite.

I wondered how long Mr. Durand would be sick, and I hoped I would still be in charge when the babies hatched. For two years I had been slipping over to Mr. Durand's loft, helping, asking hundreds of questions, and aching inside for some birds of my own. I kept thinking of how wonderful it would be to have pigeons coming home to me after a long flight, and I made a nuisance of myself asking Mom and Dad about getting a loft.

"It would be an expensive project," they'd answer, and "Sorry, not now, but maybe someday."

Every time I'd try to save my money there was some way I had to spend it—for gifts, or jeans, or something—so my owning a loft didn't ever seem to get any closer.

It was two weeks before Mr. Durand was well, and

during that time all the babies hatched. I spent so much time at the loft that Mom and Dad began calling me the Pigeon Man of Jacksonville. The parent birds fed the babies, whose mouths were always opening wide, casting around for more.

When Mr. Durand felt well enough to look at the babies, he pointed out one little cull. "The poor critter will have to be destroyed, Marty," he told me. He seemed to sense my horror. "Less cruel than letting him starve to death," he added.

I went back to the loft and picked up the cull that cried with a thin kind of whistle and flopped about vaguely. He was an ugly little thing, but I loved him!

Following Mr. Durand's instructions, I filled a bucket of water in which I was to hold the baby bird until it drowned. That was the kindest way, Mr. Durand had said, but I just couldn't go through with the operation.

"Are you willing to pay the price, Marty?" Mr. Durand asked. "You will have to chew up the grain mixture until it is milk and have that ugly mouth come into yours to eat the food."

The feeling that I'd be committing a dreadful sin if I caused the baby to die won out over the feeling of repulsion I had when I thought of that ugly little mouth in mine. Back to the loft I went, chewed and chewed until I almost felt like a parent pigeon, and then let his mouth come into mine to take the milk.

The process went on and on. At last I put him under his mother's warm body.

I got halfway across our back lawn before I lost control of my stomach. I vomited and vomited, and still could not forget the sensation of that creepy mouth in mine.

I became aware of Mr. Warriner's round head as he glared at me. Aristotle was there too, backing Mr. Warriner with his raucous bark.

During the next week I went over to the loft first thing in the morning, rushed back at noon hour, and hurried back right after school to chew and chew and feed the cull. But never at any time did I get used to the dreadful task.

The baby gained strength daily, and I felt repaid. I called him Cher, after a famous pigeon Mr. Durand had told me about. For a while Cher looked like a porcupine's relative. Then his yellowish-white feathers became white. In later weeks the ugly beak changed to a normal pigeon beak, and his half-feathers turned into true feathers.

Then one day when I was helping at the loft, Mr. Durand said, "Little Cher is yours. He wouldn't be here now if you hadn't given him so much of yourself. In fact, I hate to think of what would have become of my whole flock while I was sick. Besides that, I want you to take your pick of one of the other babies."

"Oh," I gulped, "I couldn't do that, Mr. Durand. I

didn't work that hard. I was paid enough just being able to be with them and look after them. I enjoyed it all—well, except feeding little Cher."

"Come on," Mr. Durand said, "just do as I say. Take your pick."

So I chose a baby, and I called her Ami, which was the second half of the name of the famous pigeon Mr. Durand had told me about. Dad and I made a makeshift coop, with the promise of a better one in a month or two. As we worked I kept thinking about how I wanted to take a summer job and get enough money together to add to my flock.

It was about sunset and I was putting trays of feed and water in the coop when the head of Mr. Warriner came over the top of the hedge. He hissed, "I don't want no pigeons next door to me! You hear me? No pigeons, you understand! Messy things! Burring and rumbling from daylight until dark! Get rid of them things quick—do you hear me?"

Aristotle was there as usual, his raspberry-colored tongue lolling. He seconded Mr. Warriner's sentiments with a bullying kind of bark.

All kinds of answers rushed into my throat, and looking back I wonder how I choked those hot words into silence. I turned my back on Mr. Warriner, made sure the latches were secure on the coop, placed an old blanket over it to shelter my babies, and hurried indoors.

I lay awake full of exciting thoughts that night—about Dad's driving me farther and farther from home with my pigeons so they could learn the lay of the land and find their way back home. I planned that when we went to visit my grandparents sometime, we'd let the pigeons go from their basket just as we were ready to start our trip back home. Then we'd see whether they could arrive before us. I remembered all my old longings for pigeons of my own, and I had a glowing feeling deep inside me just realizing that I now actually had the start of my flock. My last thoughts were of little Cher and Ami snuggled in their coop.

Some time later a sharp noise in the darkness woke me. Then I heard Mom and Dad moving about. I tumbled out of bed and raced to the kitchen, to find Mom and Dad outdoors. A sick horror shot clear down inside me, for I sensed that this had something to do with Cher and Ami.

The floodlights from the eaves over our kitchen showed Aristotle with wispy, downy feathers sticking around his mouth. He stood there, his tail giving the merest wag, and he had a half-guilty, half-satisfied smirk on his big wolfish face. The coop was on its side, the blanket tangled about it and the lid wide open on the grass.

Rage raced over every part of me. "That dog!" I cried. "The beast! And Mr. Warriner too!"

"Now, son, take it easy," Dad said as he put his

arm about my shoulder and stood there staring at the empty coop. Mom kissed my cheek, and I felt her arm trembling as it went around my shoulder. Her warmth made me think of the mother pigeons as they share themselves with their featherless babies. And right them I thought I knew how a newborn pigeon must feel. I saw Aristotle slink away through a break in the hedge.

I was so angry and hurt that I couldn't bring myself to tell Mr. Durand what had happened to Cher and Ami. I stayed away from him for a week. And every day, whether I was working a big math problem or diagramming a sentence or bringing home groceries for Mom, I kept getting pictures in my mind of Aristotle's smirking face with the baby pigeon feathers on it.

Some nights when I went to bed I punched my pillow and cried into it. Other times I lay awake thinking mean thoughts about Aristotle and Mr. Warriner. And in the daytime I couldn't enjoy my food or anything else, for that matter. And worst of all I couldn't talk to God, because I thought about Mr. Warriner and his dog so much.

Dad had told Mr. Warriner what Aristotle had done, but nothing had come of the conversation. All he'd done was yell at Dad that pigeons were messy things, burring and rumbling nuisances, and there ought to be a stiff law against keeping them.

Then one afternoon Mom said, "Marty, do you suppose you could manage to fix some dinner for you and Dad? I'm not feeling well. I'd hoped all the flu business was over in this neighborhood, but the way I feel I think I must be getting that Timbuktu variety I heard you talking about." Mom's smile was pretty anemic.

"You go to bed, Mom," I said. "Leave it all to the gourmet artist."

I was peeling potatoes when I looked up and saw the verse that Mom lives by: "Thou shalt love the Lord thy God with all thy heart, and . . . thy neighbor as thyself." Those last four words jumped out at me as my name does when I see it unexpectedly in print or on the chalkboard at school.

I dropped the half-peeled potato, and Mom's favorite sharp knife clattered as it hit the ceramic countertop. My knees felt like jelly as I slumped into a chair. I stared at Mom's verse for a long time. Once I got up and was about to go ask Mom if God made exceptions when there was a neighbor like ours involved. But I looked at the frying pan shaped clock above the refrigerator and saw that Dad would be home in 20 minutes, so I went back to the potatoes.

Did I ever feel trapped! Deep in my heart I knew what Mom's answer would have been about Mr. Warriner.

As I went on getting the dinner ready I realized I

was actually praying—for the first time since I'd lost Cher and Ami. "It's awfully hard to love everyone, God," I whispered. "Mr. Warriner—You know how I feel about him, and I'll never get over how I feel unless You help me. Never!"

Dad came in just then. "I was just talking with Mr. Durand," he told me. "He says Mr. Warriner is so sick with flu that the doctor put him in the hospital."

It was on my tongue to say, "Goody for him! I hope it's worse than the Timbuktu variety," but I stopped with a jerk.

After a bit, I said, "Aristotle, Dad? I suppose I ought to take over the dinner scraps when we're through."

Dad gave me a long look. "A good idea, son," he said quietly and patted my shoulder. "A mighty good idea."

As Dad started toward the bedroom I added, "Dad, do you think we could still build the permanent coop, like you said? Somewhere safe, like the attic or the tool shed?"

"I'm sure we can, son," Dad said as he gave me a big grin. "I'm sure we can."

8

A Great Team

by Everett Lee Wilhelmsen

Bruce and I stole from shadow to shadow, stopping when the December moon would escape from behind the dreary clouds that bunched up like cold, gray mice. A bitter wind raced through bare-limbed trees and whipped stinging snow into our cherry-red faces. Soon, as the shadow disappeared at the line where the bold glow of mercury lights bathed the quiet, white campus, we dashed to the dormitory and sneaked up a little-used staircase to Bruce's room.

Tile walls gleamed faintly from the hall nightlights. Only a few subdued sounds reached us through closed doors. Bruce opened his door cautiously, we stepped inside the room, and the door latch slipped quietly into place. Not a sound. We had beaten the room-check monitor!

I was about to breathe a sigh of relief when in the

darkness I thought I heard a chair creak. It wasn't Bruce who had made that sound; he was standing close enough for me to touch. Who could it be? Or was it just a branch rubbing the window? My mind whirled in the second it took to flip on the light.

The room flooded with brilliance, and I blinked at the suddenness of it. The first thing my eyes focused on was—the dean! Seated by the desk, he faced the door from the middle of the room. I looked down at my chest, wishing I'd hidden the pack of cigarettes that bulged in my shirt pocket. Immediately I found something intriguing about the rough plaster walls and ceiling, then the dark-brown tile squares under my feet. But I had to look at the dean again; I couldn't believe he was there.

"Hi, fellas," said Mr. Ashton.

"Ah-a-ah, hello, Dean." My voice, struggling in its prison of an extremely dry mouth, shook in rhythm with my trembling legs. The cigarettes shook too, and I felt certain that their rattle would bring the dean's eyes to the telltale bulge. I looked over at Bruce, who was running nervous fingers through his tangled blond curls. *I won't get any help from him in this mess*, I mused. *Not when he's just as scared as I am.*

"Where have you been?" The dean asked as he scrutinized us.

I felt sure he could smell the smoke on our heavy winter clothes. It was exasperating. If he had descended on us in a holy rage, we would have understood; but no, instead he made us terribly uncomfortable—just sitting in the chair, tipped back on two legs, while we had to stand in front of him like escaped convicts.

"We were just out for a walk," Bruce answered with a weak wave of his hand.

Then we all fell silent for what seemed an eternity. The steady drone of the gym's air blowers came through the closed windows and deepened my feeling of being in the wrong place at the wrong time. I wanted out.

After weighing all the evidence I was sure that the dean must know about my smoking. The conviction grew stronger. How could I face my parents when they came to take me home? I could imagine myself saying, "Mom, Dad, I got kicked out for smoking." The hurt on their faces, the dammed-up tears, their vain attempts to smile . . . I couldn't bear the image any longer.

"Dean?" The sound of my own voice in that tomb-quiet room startled me. "You wouldn't be here unless you knew something, would you?"

"That's right, Ed."

"Then you do know what I was doing tonight, don't you?"

"Yes, I do."

"I'm sorry, oh—I'm so sorry." I broke into tears—

hot, scalding tears. Ugly visions of a smashed future floated into my mind.

Why, oh, why had I chosen Bruce for a friend? I gazed at the floor like a cold marble statue gazing into nowhere. If I had never met Bruce, would I be in this mess?

But Bruce wasn't to blame. I was! Might as well face facts. I was always ready to do anything for recognition—for friends and acceptance. And that tendency had led me right into smoking when Bruce had casually offered me a lit cigarette after he'd inhaled a huge lungful of acrid smoke. Desire for his friendship had battled with my conscience, pulling me apart. Then had come that twist in my middle as I'd grabbed the cigarette while saying something cool like, "Sure, why not?"

Now here I stood—face-to-face with this blockbuster problem I'd created by saying "Why not?" instead of "No thanks!" I shook the hair out of my eyes and glanced at Bruce.

What he was thinking of all this I couldn't tell. His impassive, pale face, made paler by a 150-watt lightbulb glaring from the ceiling fixture, gave no hint of his thoughts. With an alcoholic mother and an unfaithful father, he had very little incentive to be good.

I had sympathized with Bruce, knowing that it was his grandmother's sacrificing that paid his tuition, that it was his grandmother who had advised him to attend this academy away from the bad influence of Los Angeles. I felt he was justified to resent being here against his wishes. Yet my good sense told me that Bruce's grandmother was right—a Christian education was something special, a privilege.

Would the dean understand our situation? Or would he see to it that Bruce and I were kicked out? Would there be a second chance for us?

"Some of your friends said they could smell tobacco in your closet, Ed." The dean's voice bounced off my throbbing head. "When I saw you and Bruce leave the dorm this evening, I thought I'd wait for you to see whether their report was correct."

"What chance have we got then, Dean?" Bruce started pulling the rumpled sheets off his bed. "You caught us, and we've had it. Guess I'd better be packing."

Mr. Ashton came down solidly with his chair. "No one said you were going to be kicked out. As a matter of fact, this whole thing will be between us. I won't report you to the principal or anyone if you promise to quit smoking and show me by your conduct that you really are trying to change."

Like a drowning person about to go down for the final time, I grabbed onto the trust held out by the dean. The understanding I had silently craved—was it really mine?

He's not being easy on us, I mused. *But he's suggesting*

to keep this quiet because he feels that by saving our reputation, saving us from embarrassment, he can help us overcome our habit without our being expelled. I can't fail him.

Suddenly the pressure of guilt and fear piled up on my shoulders vanished, and I managed my first smile of the evening. It was shaky, but it was a smile. "Here. Here are the cigarettes, Dean." I put the pack in his outstretched hand. "I quit as of tonight."

"I'm glad to hear that. How about you, Bruce?"

"Yeah. Ed just gave you all our cigarettes. I'll quit too."

"Good. I'm glad you two have made that decision. Good night, fellas." And Dean Ashton walked out of the room.

No one ever heard about that December evening when Bruce and I were caught. It has always been a secret.

Today, after finishing academy and three years in a Seventh-day Adventist college, I'm beginning to realize to what extent that one, well-controlled incident sold me on Christianity and Christian education. If I had been expelled without a second chance, I probably would never have continued my Christian schooling—or quit smoking. I'm convinced that Christ was directing my dean. He used him to show two young men a better life.

Today, I thank Jesus and Dean Ashton. They make a great team!

9

Uncle Jed's Thanksgiving Dinner

by Marvin Moore

Karen picked up the five-gallon milk can and poured a couple of quarts of fresh milk into a nursing bucket. She opened the gate to Bimbi's stall in the barn and held the bucket for her pet calf to drink. Bimbi took the large nipple at the bottom of the bucket into his mouth and sucked the milk from the pail. He opened his eyes wide as he drank, and every now and then he snorted. In almost no time the bucket was dry, but Bimbi kept sucking and sucking.

Karen laughed. "Daddy, shall I give him some more?" she asked. She turned and looked at her father pitching hay into the manger in a stall farther down the barn.

Her father came over and rumpled the hair between Bimbi's ears. He smiled. "You rascal!" he said. "If it was up to you, you'd never—" Just then the barn door rattled.

Karen felt her arm muscles tighten. She looked at her father and then at the door. The door swung back on its hinges, and Uncle Jed walked into the barn. He looked around for a few seconds while his eyes adjusted to the dark. Karen caught his glance for just an instant; then he turned and walked like a wooden soldier to the back part of the barn.

Karen felt something brush her dress. Her father had turned his back to the door and was kneeling on the floor of Bimbi's stall, as though he were examining the calf's foot.

Karen couldn't remember ever seeing her father and Uncle Jed talk, though they shared the same farm. Uncle Jed lived alone in a small house a quarter of a mile down the road from their place. Years before, there had been a quarrel, and Uncle Jed had vowed never to speak to his brother again. Karen always felt uneasy whenever she was with her father and uncle at the same time. Again tonight the air seemed tense, charged with resentment.

After Uncle Jed had gone outside, her father went back to pitching hay into the mangers. Karen left Bimbi's stall and poured milk into the bucket for another calf. Neither she nor her father spoke, but she watched him and tried to finish her work about the same time he did.

Dusk had already set in and the air felt a bit chilly as Karen and her father stepped out of the barn. She waited while he closed the door. "Daddy," she said as they walked toward the house, "why is it that you and Uncle Jed don't get along?" She waited for his reply, but for a long time she heard only the sound of his steps.

"It's a long story," he said at last.

"But isn't there anything you could do?" she asked.

"I really tried once, a long time ago," her father replied. "But I don't think Jed wants things any different. I really feel bad, but since that's the way it must be, I go along."

"But couldn't you try again?" Karen asked.

Her father shook his head. "No, my dear. It wouldn't do any good. Jed's mind is made up, and nobody can change it." They reached the house, and he held the door open for Karen.

"It smells good!" Karen said as she stepped into the kitchen.

Her mother turned around from the kettle of stew on the stove and smiled. "You're just in time," she said.

Karen's two younger brothers came in from their chores, and in a few minutes everyone sat about the table, eating and chatting happily. Karen forgot all about Uncle Jed until after supper while she and her mother were doing the dishes.

"Mother," Karen said as she picked up a plate to

dry, "why don't Daddy and Uncle Jed get along? They're brothers, and they ought to love each other. Daddy says it's a long story."

Karen's mother put the dish she had picked up back in the sink. "It's been going on a long time, dear," she said. "But it's a very simple story. So simple that it's tragic."

Karen wrinkled her eyebrows.

"Shortly after you were born, your father and Uncle Jed each had a cow. Each cow had a calf on the same night. The next day one of the calves died, and each one claims that the calf that lived was his. Your father is probably right, but I don't think it's worth the broken relationship to insist on it."

Karen finished drying a dish and set it in the cupboard. "That reminds me of Solomon and the two women with one baby," she said. "And Mother, do you remember where Solomon got the wisdom to settle that problem?"

Her mother smiled. "From the Lord."

"Then God can help solve Uncle Jed's and Daddy's problem!" Karen picked up another dish and dried it with two swishes of the towel.

Karen lay awake in bed longer than usual that night, trying to think of a way to find out whose calf had really died. But the more she thought, the more confused she became. "Dear God," she prayed before she dropped off to sleep, "I can't figure out a way to get things straightened out between Daddy and Uncle Jed. If You can, please show me."

Every day Karen thought and prayed, even in school. At home she watched Uncle Jed every chance she got, and she noticed one thing that had never occurred to her before: Uncle Jed never smiled. "He's so unhappy!" she said to herself. "I feel sorry for him, living all alone, with nobody to love him and no family to keep him company."

The last day of school before Thanksgiving arrived, and Karen still didn't have an answer to her prayer. She thought of the happy dinner she and her family would have the next day, and of the lonely time Uncle Jed would have, and she wished she could invite him to their home. But she knew she couldn't. "I guess Daddy's right," she sighed. "He wants it that way, and we can't change it."

Karen stepped off the bus after school and darted away from the dust it stirred up from the gravel road as it pulled away. She had to pass Uncle Jed's house on the way home, and she noticed that he stood by the road talking to a stranger. She tried not to act curious, but she walked past them as slowly as she dared.

"All right, why don't I come into town at ten o'-clock in the morning?" she heard Uncle Jed say.

"Oh, I wouldn't want to impose on your Thanksgiving dinner," the stranger replied.

"Don't worry about that!" Uncle Jed said. "I never

have any Thanksgiving dinner anyway. As long as I can be back by one o'clock, I don't mind at all."

Karen heard the stranger accept Uncle Jed's offer, and she walked the rest of the way home as fast as she dared without looking conspicuous. "Mother, I've got it, I've got it!" she cried as she burst through the kitchen door.

Her mother put down the pumpkin she was slicing and looked at Karen. "You've got what, dear?"

"I've decided that the calves aren't the real trouble between Daddy and Uncle Jed at all. The real trouble is that they don't love each other. Uncle Jed is so unhappy all the time—he doesn't know how to love."

"Well, I suppose that's right," her mother said. "But what can we do about it?"

"Do something nice for Uncle Jed!" Karen exclaimed.

"Do you have a suggestion?"

"Since we can't invite him to have Thanksgiving dinner with us, let's take a real nice Thanksgiving dinner to him," Karen said. "I just heard him tell someone that he'll be away from his house from ten o'clock till one tomorrow. We could sneak in and set the food on the table, and it would surprise him when he gets back." Karen felt so excited that she said everything in one breath.

Her mother thought a minute. "What if he should find out who did it?" she said. "He might be terribly angry that we went into his house."

"But, Mother, we've got to do something," Karen pleaded.

"All right," her mother said. "I'll help you get things together. But you'll have to do the actual fixing in his house by yourself. It would never do for your father or me to be there. This must be your idea and nobody else's."

Karen flew upstairs and changed her clothes. Then she came back down and helped her mother in the kitchen. She saved some of the pie filling and the crust dough for Uncle Jed's pumpkin pie. She set aside some of the loaf mix her mother had prepared, a can of cranberry sauce, a box of frozen mixed vegetables, and a package of powdered grape drink. She put everything except the frozen food into a large box and covered it with the apron she would wear.

The next morning Karen watched her uncle's house out the side window. Shortly before ten o'clock she saw him come out the front door, get into his car, and drive away. "He's gone, Mother," she said.

Her mother took the frozen vegetables and a package of margarine from the refrigerator. "Have a nice time, dear," she said, "and I'll be praying for the Lord to touch Uncle Jed's heart."

Karen hurried down the road. "I hope he didn't lock the door," she said to herself as she walked up the driveway. She stepped onto the small concrete porch and reached for the knob. "Good," she exclaimed as she pushed the door open and crossed the threshold.

She set the box of food on a chair in the kitchen and surveyed the surroundings. Dirty dishes were stacked in the sink and on the drain board, and the breakfast dishes still stood on the table. Cans of this and cartons of that were scattered about the countertop, and a couple of dirty kettles stood on the stove. "My, but this place does need a woman's attention," Karen said under her breath. She felt good to be able to help Uncle Jed.

She decided that before doing anything else, she would have to wash the dishes and straighten up the place a bit. She tied the apron around her waist, took the breakfast dishes to the counter, and started the hot water running in the sink. A half hour later, the dishes put away, she brought the food box to the counter and began preparing the dinner.

Karen poured the pie filling into the crust and spread the loaf mix in a bread pan. She checked the time that everything would need to go on the stove or in the oven in order to be ready to have it all on the table by 15 minutes before 1:00. "There is still time," she whispered. Then she swept the floor, cleaned the stove, and searched the cupboards and drawers for the best dishes to set on the table. At 11:45 she popped the pie and the roast into the oven. She spent the next few minutes setting the table and dusting the furniture.

At 12:15 Karen tore open the box of frozen mixed

vegetables, poured the peas, carrots, and corn into a heavy stainless steel pan, and set it on the stove. She had just reached for the knob to turn on the flame when she heard footsteps on the back porch.

Karen's feet froze to the floor. Her arms and legs felt like pieces of rope, and her stomach drew into a tight knot. "Oh, what shall I do, what shall I do?" she wailed under her breath. "Oh, I've ruined everything!"

The back door opened, and Uncle Jed stomped into the kitchen. For a second he seemed not to notice anything unusual. Then he sniffed the air, and almost in the same instant he turned and looked at Karen. Karen hung her head and twisted her apron in her hands. Uncle Jed stood for a long time without saying a word. Karen could feel his eyes staring at her.

"Karen, my dear," Uncle Jed said at last, "you are a better person than I am. You have shown love where all I've shown for the past 15 years is bitter hate. You know about the terrible bitterness that has existed between your father and me. Well, it's all my fault, and I know it. I want you to go back home and tell your father that if he'll come up here to see me, I'll make everything right."

Karen's heart pounded, and for a few seconds she stood rooted to the floor. "Oh, Uncle Jed!" she cried. "This is the most wonderful Thanksgiving I've ever had!" And she dashed out of the kitchen and raced down the road toward home.

10

The Best Prize

by Louise Page Craig

We're planning to have a one-mile race the day before Thanksgiving," the coach announced one morning at Springdale High. "Every boy in school is eligible. The winner will receive a 20-pound turkey. We're telling you early so you fellows can start practicing. Hope to see you all out there—and may the best man win."

"I'm going to enter that race and try my best to win," Dave told his friends. "But since we're vegetarians at our house, I don't know what I'll do with the turkey if I win it. Give it away, I guess."

Dave had wanted to go to the conference academy, but every cent of money the family could earn was needed for food and clothing. So even though he enjoyed sports, he didn't find much time for them. Besides, all the school's games and sports events were held on Friday evening or Sabbath. But here was something he could enter. Wouldn't the other kids be surprised if he won?

On the day he had enrolled at the local high school Dave had said to his parents, "Please pray for me that the Lord will give me strength to live a Christian life before the other kids."

The Lord did help, but it wasn't easy for Dave to be different. He made friends, and most of the students respected him. But there were some who loved to make his life miserable by ridiculing him.

Still vivid in his mind was the sweater episode. When he'd visited Walla Walla College not long before, he had purchased a sweater with the college insignia and name on the front. He was proud of that sweater and one morning had worn it to school. When he had headed for his locker at lunchtime, he had seen Big Butch watching him. As they passed in the hall, Butch had walked up to Dave, grabbed the sweater, and ripped it from top to bottom.

All the boys talked about the "turkey race" for weeks. They jogged on roads around the school and up and down the sidewalks in town. But after a while football, parties, and studies claimed their time, and most of them ceased jogging.

Dave kept running. He lived a mile and a half from school, and each day he jogged both ways. At first he could run only a few blocks, but as the race date neared he could run all the way to school and in the afternoon back home again without stopping.

"How's the jogging coming?" Dad asked one evening at the supper table.

"Pretty good. I'm getting better every day. All of the fellows have quit practicing except Bob Williams. He's the only one I'm worried about."

"Well, it wouldn't be much of a race without some competition."

The day before Thanksgiving Dave awoke to see large flakes of snow swirling past the window, with about two inches on the ground. "I hope they don't cancel the race," he muttered.

Upon arriving at school he was glad to find the race still scheduled. Promptly at 10:00 a.m. just about every boy in school stood at the starting line, waiting for the signal. After running four or five blocks most of them quit. Dave and Bob kept running, with Bob in the lead. "I'm gaining on him," Dave puffed. Soon he was even with Bob, and then he passed him.

The racers ran one quarter of a mile north, then turned east for another quarter of a mile, circled a teacher's car, and headed back to the starting line.

Just before he rounded the last bend—in an area out of sight of the faculty—Dave saw Butch and his buddies huddled together, making snowballs. Dave clenched his fists, looked straight ahead, and ran on as the hard missiles stung his face and blinded his vision. He closed his ears to the hoots of derision.

Then it happened. Butch shouted, "Come on, gang, let's tackle him."

Before he knew what had happened, Dave was struggling in the snow, but it was hopeless. Butch and his followers held him down as Bob ran by and won the race.

"Why did you let this happen to me, Lord? Why didn't you let me win that race?" Dave asked in his prayer that night.

But high school seniors have many things to think about besides races, so Dave pushed the disappointment of losing far to the back of his mind. The days slid rapidly by, and soon it was graduation. Dave worked all summer so he could attend Walla Walla College in the fall. He enrolled there as a theology major.

"There's nothing like going to a public high school for four years to make you appreciate a Christian college," Dave told a friend one day. It seemed to him that his college years flew by twice as fast as high school.

Dave married after graduation, and then followed the busy years of ministerial internship. Later he and his wife spent seven service-filled years in Ethiopia.

Upon returning to his homeland, Dave and his family spent a weekend in a small town in Texas where they attended Sabbath services at the little church. While participating in the lesson study, Dave felt a tap on his shoulder. He turned around, and a pleasant-faced man about his age asked, "Is your first name Dave?"

"Yes, it is."

A few minutes later there was another tap on his shoulder. The same man spoke. "Is your last name Jenson?"

"Yes."

After Sabbath school Dave went out the door to make his way to the pastor's study, having been asked to speak at the eleven o'clock service. The man who had questioned him during the lesson study stood in the foyer. He held out his hand and spoke to Dave again. "You don't remember me, do you?"

"No, I don't believe I do."

"I'm Bob Williams, the fellow who won the turkey in the Thanksgiving race at Springdale High. I didn't really win it—you did. I watched you after that and saw that you were different. You had something I wanted. I knew you were a Seventh-day Adventist and planned to go to Walla Walla College, so I decided to go there too. I couldn't go for a few years, but I finally made it. And—well—I became a Seventh-day Adventist too. I've been hoping that I would meet you someday and get a chance to thank you."

As Dave walked to the pastor's study he whispered, "Thank You, Lord, for letting me lose that race and for helping me win the best prize of all—a soul for You."

11

Springtime in the Rockies

by Dale J. Townsend

Hey, Tim, let's go inner tube riding today!" I said to my kid brother.

"Great idea, Dale."

The idea must have sprung from the weather—intoxicating, inviting. It was one of those lovely spring days in Colorado that gets into a boy's blood.

The foothills of the Rockies, light-brown much of the year except where the vital irrigation canals cut through, now looked green and blossoming. Colorado's air, always clear and dry, had a warmth that urged me on to adventure.

"Well," I prodded Tim, "what do you say?"

He hesitated. "I guess it's warm enough, but so early in the spring won't the water be awfully cold?"

"We don't have to swim, you know," I said. "We'll be riding those big tubes, hardly even touching the water. And hey, why don't we go to the canal we found this winter back on the dirt road? It doesn't have any rocks or trees or anything to splash us."

"But, Dale, it has a tunnel! Who knows what's at the other end of it? I wouldn't want to get anywhere near there—no sirree!"

"How dumb do you think I am? We can leave our bikes way above the tunnel entrance and get out well before we reach the tunnel. C'mon, let's get the tubes pumped up and tell Mom and Rudy where we're going." I jumped to my feet.

"No!" Rudy barked a few minutes later when we casually mentioned our plans.

I'd never gotten used to calling Rudy "Dad" or "Pa" or any term more appropriate to his status. Ever since Mom married him two years earlier—when I was 12—he'd seemed more like an older brother than a father—and sometimes a bossy older brother at that!

Now Rudy stood and looked at us sternly. "I saw that canal last Sabbath afternoon when I was on a walk," he told us, "and I know where it goes. There's a tunnel that takes it about a mile or two through the mountainside. The iron guard is missing at its entrance, and at the other end of the tunnel is a flume that goes into a huge, churning hole. The water just disappears under the ground, and I never did find out where it came out again. I imagine it siphons back out a few miles from there."

He would have to know about our discovery! I fumed inside. But he never took me with him on his walks or did anything with me. "You're a bother to have along," he'd mutter. "I see more by myself."

It was that way with a lot of the things I would have liked to do. He never seemed interested in having me around.

I didn't even care anymore. With his attitude, I didn't want to be with him anyway. A chilly distance had grown between us. Just stay out of each other's way—that was the key.

"Look, Rudy," I argued, "we can go way upstream and get out long before we near the tunnel. There are ladders every quarter mile or so along the edge, you might remember. We know what we are doing."

"Do whatever you want—you do anyhow." He glared. "But I'm telling you, you'd better stay far away from the tunnel entrance!"

As we were pedaling the two-mile ride uphill to the irrigation canal, Tim nodded his head toward the sky. Dark clouds crowded over the mountain range.

"Let's hurry," I urged. "Maybe we can get a ride or two before the storm hits." The dirt road met the canal where the tunnel disappeared into the mountainside.

"You know, Tim," I panted as we came to a stop, "there's a ladder right here where we could get out just as easily as anywhere. Then our bikes would be waiting for us when we get out."

"But Rudy said to 'stay far away from the tunnel entrance.'" Tim mocked Rudy's gruff-voiced order. "Isn't this a little closer than 'far away'?"

"Well, if he wants to make sure how far away we stay, let him come along and show us." I looked up at the disappearing sky. "Now, are you with me, or are you going to wait till the rain cools you off?"

Tim shrugged his shoulders and got off his bike. Grabbing our tubes, we hurried up the road. Our tennis shoes puffed up little swirls of dust, and tiny grasshoppers—the first of the year—hopped in every direction. Soon we reached a ladder leading down into the silent, swift waters.

"Well, I guess this it!" I leaned over the edge and threw in a stick.

"Boy, the rate that water's going, we'll float down a lot faster than we walked up here!" Tim gasped.

"Yeah! Isn't it great?" I shouted. "Let's go!"

We eased ourselves down the ladder and were soon floating swiftly along. But it wasn't really so great. The silence in the canal was so strange. And there was nothing to do but watch the concrete walls flash by. Where was the fun?

"Dale, my legs are about to freeze!" Tim squirmed to try to lift himself a little higher out of the water. He didn't seem to be enjoying himself much either.

Suddenly we rounded a bend, and the tunnel's dark opening loomed ahead. Tim was right—it had taken a whole lot less time than walking!

"Quick, Tim," I ordered, "you grab the ladder first, and I'll follow."

"No way! You go first and show me!"

"Hey, what's the matter with you? Get up there and get out, quick!" I gave his tube a kick. We were both floating rapidly toward that last ladder, and I didn't want to waste time holding a conference.

Tim grabbed for the ladder and with much effort pulled himself and the tube out of the frigid water. I was right behind. Together we climbed to the top of the canal and shivered there for a moment as if debating whether or not to go for another try.

"Next time, let's not wait till we get to the tunnel to decide who gets out first, OK?" I shouted at Tim.

"Well, if you weren't so bossy all the time, things might go better. It would have been your fault if we had missed the ladder!" he retorted. "That was a close one! I still don't know how we got out of there going at that speed."

"It's simple! You just paddle backward with one hand like this," I demonstrated, "and grab for the ladder with the other hand like this . . . " Letting go of my tube, I lunged for the imaginary ladder. But just then my tube, freed of my grasp, rolled down the slope and over the edge of the canal.

"Yikes—there goes my tube!" I jumped for it and fell into the swirling waters.

"Dale, stop! You're heading right for the tunnel! Dale! No!" Tim was jumping up and down and screaming.

"Help me! I can't stop!" I was standing, but although the water was only thigh deep, it was so swift that I couldn't stand still. Even with my tennis shoes digging the rough bottom, I was shoved along. "No! Help me! Stop me!"

The deep, dark mouth of the tunnel loomed right over me. I tried to clutch the canal walls, but all I accomplished was to scrape off the tips of my fingernails. The last thing I heard as I was sucked into the tunnel's black interior was a final wail from Tim: "Dale . . . Noooooooo!"

Blackness—horrible, silent, cold blackness—engulfed me. Then a small round light about the size of a baseball loomed ahead. I realized that it was the end of the tunnel, growing larger by the minute.

Hard as I tried, I couldn't stop myself from being swept along. The tunnel walls were straight and its floors slippery. It was no use. The circle of light rapidly loomed larger and brighter.

"What's going to happen to me?" My voice only echoed off the interior of the tunnel. "No! Not me! Oh, God, help me somehow!"

Then a new fear gripped me. Would God help me? I remembered Rudy's glare—was God glaring too? I had disobeyed my stepfather.

Rudy! I could just hear him when they found my body—if they ever did! "He thought he knew so much!" he'd say. "I warned him not to go there! Well, he learned his lesson—the hard way!" The thought terrified me. "He hates me!" I screamed.

I was so engrossed with my own emotions and frantic efforts to stall my speed through the tunnel that I had no thoughts to spare for my terrified brother back on the edge of the canal. Some faint hope might have reached me had I known the speed record he was breaking racing home, or heard the volume of his shouts that roused the household: "Dale's in the tunnel! Hurry! Help! Dale's gone!"

Evidently Rudy lost no time gathering up a length of rope and roaring off in the truck, his sharp mind calculating the few minutes it would take me to get through the mile-long tunnel. Unfortunately, no matter how he figured it, he always concluded that I'd already met my death in the underground siphon at the other end. But he knew exactly where that tunnel came out. It was more than coincidence that he had stumbled onto it a few days before.

"I don't want to die!" I shouted. Mindful only of my own predicament, I thrashed and struggled against the unending force of gray water bearing me ever closer to the widening circle of light. My tube, about 100 feet ahead of me, bobbed in the center of it. Suddenly I saw it drop. No! The end! I couldn't go over!

"O Lord, stop me!" I had tried before to stop, but now I struggled like a maniac. In my efforts I tore my tennis shoes to shreds on the concrete bottom and ground my feet raw. My fingers clawed the rough walls for a hold until they were split and bleeding, but the water's pull prevented any stopping. A dull roar—at the flume—was breaking the tunnel's eerie silence. Just at the edge of disaster, my fingers slipped into a crack—the joint between the tunnel wall and the flume wall. And I stopped.

The force of the water was unbelievable. Its icy chill splashed over my entire numb body. I turned my head around and looked out of the tunnel. Cows grazed peaceably on the far side of the green mountain valley. Colorado was teeming with life, and I was teetering on the edge of death.

"Help! Help!" My aching muscles cramped. I couldn't hang on long, and this temporary postponement of death was just taunting me. I turned back and cringed against the liquid monster.

"O Lord, help me! My hold is so weak. Send me an angel, please? Just one angel to lift me out of here. That's all it would take. One angel, Lord—"

"Dale! Hang on a little more; I've got a rope!" It was Rudy! I turned my head enough to see his frame silhouetted against the blue sky at the mouth of the tunnel. He clutched a rope in one hand and with the other clung to the barbed wire fence surrounding the dreadful flume. Soon the rope dangled temptingly near, about five feet away, but past the end of the canal.

"That's as close as I can get it!" Rudy yelled above the roar of the flume. "You'll have to grab it on your way over. Ready?"

"Here I come!" I had no choice but to let go. As the angry gray water hurled me over the edge, I grabbed for the small strand of rope. I caught its last few inches.

Slowly Rudy began to pull me up. I clutched the rope with stiff fingers, never even feeling it tighten deeply into my cold skin. Shutting my eyes, I concentrated on one thing—hanging on.

Then strong arms grabbed me, pulling me out of the canal and to my feet. Opening my eyes, I saw Rudy's strained face looking into mine.

There was a moment of silence, and then Rudy threw warm, strong, fatherly arms around me as he choked. "Oh, Dale, you're alive! We made it!"

"I—I'm so glad! It was so s-s-scary!" Teeth chattering, I drank in the comfort of my sure haven. "Oh, Rudy, I'm so sorry I didn't listen to you." I hugged him back with aching, weary arms.

Rudy loved me. God loved me.

Feeling, warm feeling, was coming back all over me. The good solid world around me was real. Colorado was teeming with life. So was I!

12

"Just Kids"

by Mary Duplex

Mara stopped in the doorway of her brother's fifth-grade classroom. Her left hand felt slippery and damp as she gripped the leash and the stiff U-shaped leather handle of Gretchen's harness.

Why did I let myself get talked into this so soon? she thought. *If only Alex had asked my permission before he told his class about me.*

She became aware of hushed whispers. *You have to get over being so self-conscious,* she told herself sternly. *After all, it isn't you they're interested in. It's Gretchen they want to see and learn about.*

Mara took a deep breath. "Forward," she said softly. The guide dog moved obediently into the room.

The smell of chalk dust and books and freshly sharpened pencils brought the familiar room clearly into her mind. Six years ago she had been a student here herself.

Footsteps came toward her. "Mara, how nice to see you again," Mrs. Boyd said. "The students have been looking forward to your visit."

Mara smiled. Mrs. Boyd sounded just the same. "I'm glad to be here," Mara said. "I hope I can tell the class what they want to know."

"I'm sure you can," the teacher said. "Step over here by my desk. The children can gather around so they can all see."

"Forward," Mara said. There was a flurry of quick steps and a shifting of chairs.

Mara let go of Gretchen's harness and held the leash lightly in her hand. The big German shepherd settled down at her feet. "I think it would be best if you asked questions," Mara said. "Ask anything you like."

"Did you get your dog right after—after . . ." The girl's voice trailed off.

Mara smiled. "After I became blind?" she replied, finishing the question. "No. I've been blind for almost two years, but I've had Gretchen for only six weeks."

"Where did you get the dog?" a boy asked.

"From the Seeing Eye Institute. I applied for a dog a long time ago and was placed on the waiting list. When they told me Gretchen was available, I flew to the International Guiding Eyes school in California to get her."

"Didn't you get to pick her out yourself?" someone asked.

Mara shook her head. "That's done by the people at the school. The dogs are schooled for three months by Seeing Eye trainers before we get them. They're taught to obey commands, or to disobey any command that will put a blind person in danger. They learn how to cope with traffic and any other situation that a blind person walking down the street might find difficult. Shortly after I arrived at the institute, Gretchen was given to me. We went through a four-week training course together so I could learn how to let Gretchen be my eyes."

"Does she ever let you bump into anything?" There was a note of doubt in the boy's voice.

Mara smiled. "No. Having Gretchen is almost like being able to see again. I can go places and do things I never expected to be able to do."

"What happens when you want to go someplace dogs aren't allowed?" someone asked.

"Guide dogs can go almost everywhere," Mara said. "On buses, in restaurants, in stores, anyplace their masters need to go."

"Even school?" a boy asked. Everyone laughed.

"Yes, even school," Mara said. "Now that I have

Gretchen, I've been able to enroll in a special business course."

"Are guide dogs expensive?" The question came from somewhere to her right.

"They cost several hundred dollars apiece. A lot of work goes into their care and training."

"How do they know which dogs will be good guide dogs?" This time Mara recognized the voice. It was Alex's friend Jim.

"The dogs are chosen, Jim, by the Seeing Eye institute when they're puppies," she answered. "Then they're placed in homes and raised by boys and girls like yourselves until they're old enough to be trained. A lot of the dogs are raised by 4-H members."

"It must be tough to give them up," Jim said. "Why doesn't the institute raise them in kennels?"

"The dogs are raised in a family atmosphere because then it's easier for them to adjust to the homes of their new owners," Mara explained. "Any more questions?"

No one spoke. Mara touched the Braille watch on her wrist. "I'd better be going. I don't want to be late for my own classes."

"Thank you for coming," Mrs. Boyd said. The air was again filled with whispers as Mara left the room.

Alex was home by the time Mara arrived that afternoon. "Everybody thought your visit was really neat," he reported. "After you left, the class talked it over, and we decided to try to raise money to help buy a guide dog for someone."

"That's a wonderful idea," Mara said. She sat down on the sofa and unfastened Gretchen's leash and harness. "How do you plan to go about it?"

Alex dropped down beside her. "Well, to start with, we're going to collect aluminum cans for recycling, and the girls want to have a bake sale." His voice was filled with enthusiasm. "And we're going to put some collection cans around the school so the other kids can help if they want to, and we're going to make things to sell. There are lots of ways we can raise money."

Mara laughed and rumpled his hair. "Every little bit helps. Whatever you raise will be appreciated by someone. Good luck!"

As fall faded into winter, Mara got used to Gretchen detouring around big plastic bags of aluminum cans on the porch and Alex and Jim working away in Alex's room. She almost forgot about the class project as she became more and more absorbed in her own classes.

The first faint smell of spring mingled with the wintry breeze as Mara and Gretchen walked the last few blocks from the bus stop one afternoon. There was a bounce in Mara's step. Her instructor had just assured her that there would be a job waiting for her when she graduated in a few short weeks. Her dream of independence was about to come true.

Gretchen stopped for a traffic signal. Mara waited impatiently for it to change.

Then the people around her began to move. "Forward," she said. They stepped off the curb.

Suddenly Gretchen barred Mara's path. The dog pressed her body against Mara's knees and forced her to take a step backward. Mara heard a car coming as Gretchen pressed harder. Before she could take another backward step, the car roared past. The harness and leash were jerked from her hand, and Mara staggered and fell against the curb. Angry voices shouted as the car sped around the corner.

A gentle hand touched Mara's shoulder. "Are you all right?" the man asked.

"I think so," Mara said as she groped for Gretchen's harness. Suddenly a chill of fear ran down her spine. Gretchen had never before left her side when she had taken a spill. She had always been right there licking her in the face. "Where's my dog? Is she all right?"

"I'm sorry," the man said sympathetically. "There's nothing we can do for her. Is there someone you'd like me to call?"

Numb with shock, Mara gave him her mother's name and phone number.

Spring arrived with the soft warmth of the sun and the fragrance of growing things, but with

Gretchen gone Mara found little joy. For her there were no more classes. The business school across town had been easy to reach with Gretchen's help. But it was a distance she could never manage with her white cane. Alex was still in school, and with her mother working there was no one to take her there and pick her up each day.

"I got the mail," Alex called when he came in from school one day. "Hey, you got a letter, Mara. Want me to read it to you?"

Mara shrugged. "I suppose so. It's probably from the institute."

Alex ripped the envelope open. "It's from the local Seeing Eye society. It says:

"Dear Miss Moore:

"It has been brought to our attention that you have lost your guide dog through an unfortunate accident. Recently we received a donation of $670.23 from the fifth-grade children of Emerson Elementary School. Since the children were inspired by your visit to their classroom last fall, we have set aside part of the funds they raised to replace your guide dog. Arrangements are being made at the Seeing Eye school."

Mara gasped. "Oh, Alex! Did your class really raise that much money?"

"Sure," Alex said. "I told you about it several times, but I guess you were feeling so bad about los-

GGGS-4

ing Gretchen that you didn't pay much attention. We—"

Mara didn't wait to hear the rest. She threw her arms around Alex and hugged him so tightly that it took his breath away. "You're just kids! I never dreamed you would stick to such a project."

"Hey, cut it out, will ya?" Alex wiggled out of her grasp. "We may be just kids, but we found out there are a lot of ways we can help people."

On the last day of school Mara stood in front of Mrs. Boyd's class once more. A young German shepherd stood quietly beside her. She swallowed hard at the lump in her throat. "I want you all to meet Teesha, the dog you worked so hard to buy. And I want to thank you all for giving me back my future."

13

Operation Deep Freeze

by Daniel J. Fahrbach

Tom and Rick were not feeling philosophical about the Ten Commandments the afternoon they stole four boxes of Eskimo Pies and Klondike bars from the academy cafeteria. They were thinking how clever they were.

On that Friday the last snows of the Wisconsin winter lay in heaps across the campus like dinosaur bones in a desert. Bare cornfields stretched miles to the horizon, leaving the academy campus isolated. A visiting preacher had once said they were like the children of Israel wandering in the wilderness. It felt like that. And there wasn't a Dairy Queen or an ice-cream shop of any kind in sight.

It had been Rick's idea. They were spending their second afternoon defrosting the cafeteria's walk-in freezer—cracking chunks of ice off the walls and shelves, loading the slabs into a wheelbarrow, and dumping the stuff outside. The frozen foods loading the shelves included stacks of ice-cream desserts.

"Tom, I've been thinking."

An interesting—possibly bad—sign, Tom noted.

"How long has it been since Miss David served an ice-cream dessert? Haven't we been getting a lot of pudding lately?"

"Pudding and tapioca," responded Tom with caution as he pried loose another slab of ice.

The freezer door was shut. Rick blew on his hands. "Tom, do you remember the first signs of ice-cream deficiency?"

"Is that something I missed in health class?"

"First, the deprived victim develops an intense craving for the essential nutrient. This is followed in several weeks by a progressive decline in mental ability, and the victim becomes less and less responsible for his actions. Finally, there's a pitiful collapse, and the sufferer begins eating yogurt."

"What's your point, doctor?"

"We need ice cream. Our friends need ice cream."

Rick's plan was to smuggle out several boxes of ice cream in the wheelbarrow. They could place the boxes in the bottom, cover them with ice, and wheel them past Miss David, the cook. Once outside the back door, they could bury the ice cream in a snowbank. Later, like Bluebeard and his pirates, they would come back under the cover of night for the treasure.

The first load of two blue boxes of Eskimo Pies went out without a hitch. This success was followed by two boxes of Klondike bars. Rick made a giddy joke about how the freezer was really a bank vault and the Klondike bars were really gold bars. Tom began planning an invitation list for a social occasion to take place later that night.

The operation proceeded flawlessly until several freshman girls, who were washing pans in the kitchen, overreacted to Rick's generous gift of three ice-cream bars. Miss David caught them. They were quick to confess, and half an hour later Tom and Rick were seated on uncomfortable chairs in the principal's office.

Elder K was punching a number on the telephone. "Tom," he said, "I know how disappointed this will make your mother."

Rick was trying to explain that they were really just practicing for smuggling Bibles into forbidden countries, a career he hoped to get into after graduation. Tom knew this story sounded lame. It wasn't even funny. Stealing. It was just a few ice-cream bars, but now Elder K was talking to his mother about suspension from school.

Tom looked up as Elder K held the telephone receiver toward him. "Mom, it seemed funny at the time." Tom paused and listened to 200 miles of long-distance silence. "I guess you'd have had to have been there." He handed the receiver back across the desk and stared dumbly at Elder K's golf putter leaning in the corner. So this was the life of crime.

Elder K tried to reach Rick's parents. He was having trouble. Rick's mother and father lived in different states since the divorce. Rick kept giving Elder K new phone numbers to try. He had them all memorized. His mom's at home and at work. His mom's special friend. The same for his father. His grandparents. No one was home.

"I'm sorry, Rick." Tom looked over at his accomplice.

"It was silly. My idea."

"No, I mean about your parents."

"Oh." Tom had never talked to Rick about his parents splitting up, and here in the principal's office seemed a funny place to start. "Yeah, I'm sorry too."

Elder K finally gave up trying to call. He looked tired. *Nothing a hot-fudge sundae couldn't fix,* Tom thought dryly.

Luckily, it was late Friday afternoon.

"Young men," Elder K began, "you have displayed the attitude that the rules are something to trifle with—that this is a game. We take this matter seriously. I ask you, What is the difference between stealing ice cream and stealing money?"

From the corner of his eye, Tom saw Rick's left

foot twisting and turning—a little athletic motion he brought to bear on especially difficult math problems or conversations with girls.

"I am considering suspending you both for a week," Elder K concluded.

A week! That would mean missing two dates with Susan and the basketball final next Sunday. It would mean a lot of extra homework. It would mean evenings alone with his disappointed mom.

"But as it is Friday afternoon," Elder K said, showing them to the door, "we will have to wait until Sunday's faculty meeting for the final decision. Enjoy your Sabbath."

Saved by the Sabbath! Oh, blessed day of rest.

When Tom and Rick walked into the cafeteria for the Friday evening meal of chili, cottage cheese, and hot cinnamon rolls, there was a crackling of applause. Which helped a little, but mostly made them think how much they didn't want to be suspended.

It was later that night as Tom was staring at the ceiling above his bunk that he started getting philosophical about the Ten Commandments. He started like this: Most of the time, Sabbath seemed like a day of don'ts and can'ts. But this Sabbath was totally different. It had opened up in front of Rick and him like a place of refuge. Without Friday night, at this moment they would probably be before the faculty committee, pleading for grace. It seemed odd that a law spoken thousands of years ago in rolling thunder could have any bearing on something as silly as the case of two twentieth-century ice-cream thieves.

"Tom," Rick interrupted his thoughts, "do you really think we'll be suspended?" Rick was playing a Del Delker song again and again on the stereo. The words went something like "I just live from day to day . . ."

Tom sighed deeply. "I'm hoping the faculty members will show a sense of humor. I don't know. Maybe over Sabbath Elder K will change his mind."

"I'm sorry if I talked you into this caper."

"Forget it." Tom paused. "Rick, where will you go if we do get suspended? Your mom's or your dad's?"

"I don't even want to think about it."

"Do you want to talk about your parents? Their divorce, I mean."

"I don't know if it helps. It makes me mad. It hurts. It's worse than they say." Rick restarted the Del Delker song, and for a long time they listened to the music. When they were both thinking about it, maybe it was as good as talking about it.

Through the window Tom could see that it had started to snow.

"Hey, want to make some snow cones? You find some of that Swiss Miss. I'll get the snow."

Tom put on his Levi's jacket and went down the hall and out the side door. The campus, with the lights in the girls' dorm windows and from the lamp-post, glowed in the swirling snow like one of those paperweights. Snowflakes melted on his cheeks.

The Ten Commandments are more than rules in a game, he was thinking. *They are a code of conduct designed to protect us from hurting ourselves and each other.* That was true about stealing, coveting, and lying; the ice-cream caper showed that. It was true about the Sabbath. And it was true—as Rick knew better than he did—about the seventh commandment, the one about families staying together.

Tom didn't know how Sunday's faculty meeting would turn out. Maybe he would tell them what he had been thinking about.

Tom bent down to scoop up some snow. For just a second he felt like one of the Israelites collecting manna under the shadow of Mount Sinai. He filled two cups.

14

"I'm Going to Get You!"

by Jane Chase

peered over my father's shoulder through the frosty window glass. An old rusty car was parked in our driveway. Its tire tracks on the snowy country road wove back and forth like a snake. A man in a thick parka, fur-topped boots, and faded jeans stepped out of the car. He slammed the door behind him and shifted the rifle in his hands.

"I told you I'd be back," he yelled. His voice slurred, and his breath rose like white fog in the night air. He tramped through the deep snow toward the house, his steps wavering like his tire tracks. "I'm going to get you if it takes all night," he bellowed, cocking his gun.

"Turn out the lights, Ma," my father said.

Mother flicked off the living room lights, then the kitchen light and the hall light. With the house pitch-black, the man could no longer see inside for a clear target. Outside, everything looked brighter. Moonlight shimmered on the fields of snow and glinted off the man's rifle.

I took hold of my father's arm. "Who is he?" I asked in a whisper. "What does he want?"

"That's Bill Grier," my father answered. "He was in the store this afternoon demanding drugs. Prescription medicine. But he didn't have a prescription."

My father is a pharmacist and sells medicine to anyone who comes into his store with a doctor's prescription.

"Why doesn't he go to the doctor and get one?" I asked.

"Because no doctor will give him one. He isn't sick. He's addicted." My father crossed the room to the other window as Mr. Grier stomped around the house. "He was angry when he left this afternoon, but I didn't think he was so upset that he'd come after me here."

"I know you got drugs in there!" Mr. Grier yelled.

As Mr. Grier tramped to the back of the house, my father said, "Jane, go to your room. Ma, get the gun."

I stopped when I heard those words. Get the gun? The only reason my father owned a gun was to frighten the occasional wolf that drifted too close to our rural Minnesota home.

I went to my room, but not all the way. Instead, I crouched on the stairs and peeked through the banister rails.

My mother disappeared into the bedroom and came out carrying the gun. She gave it to my father. I heard the sliding of the rifle's bolt as my father slipped a shell into the weapon.

"I'm going to call the police," she said. My father nodded.

My heart pounded and my hands were sweating as I gripped the banister. Mr. Grier's voice came from behind the house.

"You let me in or else!" I heard him curse as he circled back to the front. Then I heard my mother talking to the police, asking them to send someone out right away. Her voice was calm and steady.

Ka-BOOM! The sound of a gunshot thundered through the house, and glass shattered. I dropped flat on the stairs, my face buried in my arms. I was so scared that I thought I was going to lose my supper. I heard the telephone receiver clatter on the kitchen floor. I couldn't look. What if Mr. Grier had shot my father?

"Dear God, please . . ." was all I could pray. I peeked out. My father still stood by the broken window, the rifle in the crook of his elbow. I could see his breath as the winter air drifted inside. He was breathing fast, shallow. I couldn't see any blood, but the side of my father's shirt was torn. I knew then that his quick breathing was from being scared, not hurt.

"Thank You, God," I whispered.

My father pointed the gun out the window and toward the sky. My stomach twisted in a knot. Suddenly my father fired the gun into the air. The shot rang clean and crisp.

From my spot on the stairs I couldn't see Mr. Grier. But I heard his curses mixed with the sound of his running steps crunching the snow. His car started with a roar. My heart beat faster as I heard approaching sirens. I left my hiding place and went to stand by my father. Holding his arm in my shaking hands, I looked out the shattered window.

Mr. Grier had made a U-turn in our plowed driveway, but two police cars sped up the long drive and slid to a halt, blocking his way. The officers got out, guns drawn. They made Mr. Grier get out of the car and handcuffed him.

"You both stay here while I talk to them," my father said. He grabbed his coat and handed the rifle to my mother. "Take care of this," he told her. I could see my mother's fingers tremble as she took the weapon.

I watched my father hike through the deep snow on the driveway. With Mr. Grier in the backseat of one of the police cars, the officers and my father talked. I couldn't hear what they said, but they talked for a long time. Finally the officers got in their cars and drove away. My father stood there a minute and then came back inside.

Mother and I met him in the kitchen.

"What happened?" my mother asked. "What did they say?"

My father sat down and heaved a long sigh.

"I told them everything, starting with this afternoon. They're going to hold Bill tonight and take statements tomorrow, after he's had a chance to sober up a bit."

"I hope they lock him up for a long time," I said. "He's a scary, horrible man." Even though the danger was over, I still felt trembly inside. "What if he had shot you, Dad?"

My father smiled and held out his arms. "Come here, Jane," he said gently.

I went to him and crawled onto his lap. He wrapped his arms around me. I could feel the cold air that still clung to his coat.

"Bill isn't really a horrible man. He just has some problems. He needs Jesus more than he needs to be locked up."

"Let's pray for him right now," my mother said. She came and sat next to us. Then she took one of my father's hands as he held me in his arms.

"Dear Jesus," my father began, "please be with Bill tonight and wrap him in Your arms of love. Show him that drugs and alcohol aren't the answers to his problems. You are. Give him peace and the joy that comes with trusting in You. And help me to love Bill as You do. Amen."

Silence filled the kitchen. I looked up at my father. "How could you love Mr. Grier? He tried to shoot you."

My father smiled quietly. "I can't love him on my own. But with Jesus in me I can."

Years later I asked my father about that winter night. He hardly even remembered it. But I will never forget that night and the lesson my father taught me—how to love my enemies.

15

House in Flames

by Jennifer Jill Schwirzer

One spring evening my kid brother, Scotty, threw open my bedroom door without knocking. His eyes looked like alarm clocks as he blurted out, "Sue Cook's house is burning down!"

Sue and I had lots of mischievousness and time with little supervision—a deadly combination. Add to that the fact that we were not committed to God in any way, and you have a formula for disaster.

A really stupid thing Sue and I did with our spare time was smoking cigarettes. And one day when we were passing a cigarette back and forth between each other, we heard one of the side doors in her house open and close. Scared of being caught, we ran to see who it was and found only Heidi, the dog.

When we returned to the couch where we'd been smoking, however, we discovered that we had dropped the burning cigarette into the side of the couch, and it had burned its way through into the springs, where we couldn't possibly retrieve it. We poured a couple of glasses of water on the hole, sure that the water would go into the couch and quench the fire. After that we sprayed some air freshener, and then Sue went to meet her family somewhere and I went home.

It was later that night that Scotty burst into my bedroom and told me about Sue's house being on fire.

I immediately knew what had started the fire. Propelled by guilt and fear, I raced to her house, riding my bike, then throwing it down to run the last few blocks until I reached the pristine suburban road where Sue lived.

A mob of people jammed the street and yard, but I could still see the black smoke billowing out of the windows. The house was brick, or else it would have burned to the ground. *Someday I'm going to make enough money to pay them back for burning their house down*, I vowed inwardly. I hated the feeling of being under a cloud of condemnation.

I ran to the backyard, where Sue was surrounded by a group of girls. Putting my tearstained face in hers, I looked her in the eye, begging without words for some comfort. I would have confessed right then and there to the police and our parents if Sue had given me the go-ahead. Instead, she hissed, "Don't tell anyone!"

I was forced to choose between honesty and friendship. I chose friendship.

Somehow I couldn't cross Sue's will and risk losing her. So we pretended we didn't know anything about the disaster. There was talk about an electrical fire, a short in the wall. Who knew? House fires happen.

It worked for about a year. Sue's family moved into the Holiday Inn for a while, then into a house in another suburb about 20 minutes away. She attended a different school, but we remained friends. Perhaps part of our bond was our common secret and our common fear of discovery.

Sue's dad was, of all things, a lawyer. I thought of him as a cold, distant judge who would punish us severely if he ever found out. Then one day he found a note I had written to Sue that divulged the whole matter. He arranged a meeting with Sue and me to discuss the matter. Doomsday had arrived.

The verdict was worse than I could have imagined: I had to tell my mom.

My mother and I were sitting in her station wagon after a trip to Brown-Port Shopping Center on a cold gray day.

"Mom? Remember Cooks' fire?" I whispered.

"Yes." Mom eyes darted around in anticipation of bad news.

"I was responsible for it."

I still feel sick thinking about how much pain those words brought to my mom's heart. My punishment was watching her cry—worse than the electric chair, I think.

My mom and dad stayed friends with the Cooks for years after the fiery incident, believe it or not. By then I was a young adult and had even made a couple of music CDs. Mr. Cook called my mom one Christmas and asked her to sell him two of my CDs as a Christmas present for Sue. Mom called and asked me to send them.

"And send a bill for the CDs to Mr. Cook," she added.

My mouth dropped open. "Mom, I can't bill Mr. Cook. I burned his house down, remember?"

"Oh, don't be silly, Jennifer!" Mom scolded. "He doesn't hold that against you!"

But how could I know for sure? I decided to send him a note along with the CDs. "Dear Mr. Cook," I wrote. "Please take these CDs free of charge. Consider this a down payment on the great debt that I owe you."

What he wrote back still takes my breath away: "Considering your comment about the great debt that you owe me . . . I never considered, even for a moment, that you owed me anything."

As I read those words, my mind spun in circles trying to grasp them. All the ideas I had of Mr.

Cook—the lawyer, the legalist, the grudge-bearing judge—fell flat as a different Mr. Cook emerged, treading the rest of them underfoot. Mr. Cook, the forgiver.

How could it be? I had spent years feeling indebted when he never considered, even for a moment, that I owed him anything.

And because of Mr. Cook, I view God differently, too. I realize that I don't have to cast guilty glances over my shoulders, hoping to avoid Him. I don't need to make little offerings to Him, thinking it's a down payment on a debt I can never pay. He's forgiven me—and you. He's already canceled the debt we owe Him. He calls it grace. I call it amazing.

16

The Cucumber Squad

by Randy Fishell

Wow—there's a whole lot of cukes in your patch!"

My chest swelled with pride at the comment of my friend Lennie as we looked around at the growing fruits of our summer labors. It had been a while since Lennie had seen our family's summer project, and his comment reminded me that our hard work was about to pay off big.

"Now you just have to make sure nobody steals any of those cucumbers," Lennie cautioned.

"Wh-what do you mean?"

"Well," Lennie continued, "you never know. Some crook might drive by here and see all these cucumbers and think, *I'll just slip over here tonight and pick this patch clean.* The next morning you'll come out and find nothing but leaves and stems.

And then you can kiss your cash crop goodbye."

Cucumber thief? I'd been so busy hoeing and complaining that I'd never stopped to think that our entire operation went unguarded between sundown and sunrise. While my family was fast asleep, dastardly Vince Levine or some other thief could be cleaning us out, slick as a pickle! Just as Lennie said, the heist could be over before we woke up!

Earlier in the season I wouldn't have been so concerned. But now, with the patch covered in lush foliage and laced with bright-yellow blossoms, I had too much invested in the project to let it slip away without a fight. Recruiting the Michigan National Guard to patrol the perimeters of the patch was an option, but about as likely as Mom and Dad calling the project off and suggesting we spend the rest of the summer vacationing in Hawaii.

As we pondered our potential business-destroying predicament, my eyes drifted over to the lone cherry tree silhouetted high on the hill near our house. "The tree fort!" I exclaimed. "We can sleep there tonight and watch for cucumber crooks!"

Lennie, who had nothing to gain personally, nevertheless caught the spirit. Glancing up at the tree fort, he smiled and slowly nodded. "That's a pretty good idea. I'll ask my folks if I can bring my sleeping bag—and my gun."

Lennie had recently received a Crossman BB gun

for his birthday. While its precision was hardly that of a heat-seeking missile, scoring a hit was less important than the feeling of security it would lend us tree fort dwellers come darkness. There was another benefit attached to the weapon: its rapid-fire popping sound would cause the thief to believe that someone had arisen in our house to make a late-night bowl of popcorn. That alone should be good enough to scare the bad guy away.

"Here comes my sleeping bag," I called out to Lennie, who awaited my toss overhead. With the sun dipping low on the western horizon, we were stocking up for the big stakeout. I grabbed hold of a lower tree limb and swung up to catch the next branch.

My older brother, Dave, had decided to join our regiment, fearful of missing out on any late-night entertainment this experience might bring. "Mom sent these along," he announced, holding out a plate of chocolate-chip cookies. A more committed group of night watchmen might have held the sweet treats in reserve for launching at the cucumber culprit should the BBs run out. But we scarfed the cookies down in hopes of sweet dreams.

"OK," Lennie announced, assuming command, "what we need to do is each take a watch." I waited for him to hand a Timex to us, but he just kept talking. "We'll each stay awake for 15 minutes while the other two guys sleep. Then the one on duty will wake up the next person, and the first guard will hit the sack. We'll keep changing places until sunrise. Got it?"

"Yeah, OK," I agreed.

"Sure," Dave nodded.

Suddenly I realized that one highly important question remained unanswered. "Hey, Lennie," I asked, "what exactly do we do if we spot the pickle-lifter? I mean, it's not like we can just shout, 'Put up your cukes!' or something."

A sly smile crossed Lennie's face. He reached underneath his sleeping bag and pulled out the BB gun. Dave's and my eyes grew wide as our big-shot compatriot held the weapon high. "Does this answer your question?" he said cockily.

"Ohhh . . . gotcha," we both said, nodding.

With our confidence running thick as tree sap, we negotiated the watch rotation. With Lennie on duty first, Dave and I slipped into our sleeping bags.

The plan went off like clockwork far into the night or, more honestly, until after I'd taken over and stared into a moonlit, motionless field of brain-dead vegetables for about six minutes. With Lennie and Dave slumbering blissfully nearby, the entire scene was more potent than the strongest sleeping pill available, with or without a prescription.

"Dave," I whispered, "are you awake?"

"I don't think so."

"Look, I can't stay awake," I said hesitantly. "And this tree fort is too crowded. I'm going inside." For just a moment I thought I saw Lennie reach under his sleeping bag.

Dave propped himself up on one elbow. "Oh, all right. Lennie and I'll cover for you."

"Hey, thanks," I said with a weary smile. I climbed down the tree fort's ladder steps and soon found myself in my own bed, snug as a bug in a no-insecticide cucumber patch.

The next morning, after a fabulous night's sleep, I sped out to check the results of the previous night's efforts. I lifted a vine and peeked underneath. The plant was loaded with cukes! A repeat performance in several other locations told me that our crop was safe. Racing back to the tree fort, I scampered up its limbs to salute the cucumber squad.

"Hey, guys," I shouted to the two semicomatose figures on the floor of the tree fort, "the cukes are still there!"

The mumbling and lack of positive response told me that the dynamic duo's physical and emotional reserves had been spent during the ordeal. Without further comment I retreated, lest Lennie consider me fodder for early-morning target practice.

Eventually something important dawned on me: Saving the cukes wasn't the most important thing that happened that night. Dave's act of grace—letting me out of night watchman duty and still allowing me to share in the end-of-summer profits—was a pretty big deal.

Of course, it wasn't as big as Jesus' gracious act on Calvary, the one that paved the way for sorry sinners to spend forever with Him. Satan played his tricks in the Garden and figured that humans would never reap a harvest called heaven. But he didn't know that Jesus would one day say, "Whoever does God's will is my brother" (Mark 3:35), and then perform an astonishing act of grace.

Thank heaven for really good brothers.

17

Witness in the Courtroom

by Jeane Burgess Ewald

André dear," Martha said seriously one evening, "I wish you wouldn't work quite so hard." Her young husband had come in exhausted from a long day of work on their small farm in Hungary.

André Kovack stopped washing his face so abruptly that the soapy water dripped off his chin and splashed onto Martha's clean-scrubbed kitchen floor.

"Why, bless you, my dear," he said heartily, a grin spreading slowly across his rugged features. "I'm not working too hard. Sure, I get tired, but a good night's rest takes care of that."

He returned to his face-washing with renewed energy, pausing at last to dry on the clean white towel. Tantalizing odors drifted in from the oven. Martha was a wonderful cook. Big puffy loaves of bread, crunchy bread sticks filled with cottage cheese and egg salad, fluffy white mashed potatoes, and a tossed salad awaited them. André's mouth watered.

André paused to pat his son, little André, on the head and to swoop baby Anna high into the air. Her delighted shrieks filled the tiny cottage. André deposited the little girl in her high chair while young André climbed up onto his chair. They all bowed their heads as André prayed, "Our heavenly Father, we thank Thee for this food. Bless the hands that prepared it."

After supper was finished and the dishes were done, André and Martha prayed with the children and tucked them into bed, then lovingly placed the old family Bible back on its shelf. They did their best to teach their children to follow God.

Sabbaths were especially precious to this Seventh-day Adventist family. Though they often invited their neighbors to worship with them, few came, and those only occasionally. The Kovacks were well-respected in the community. "But it just doesn't seem necessary to be so different," the neighbors sometimes said.

Then the war came. The news that filtered back to the tiny village week by week was disheartening. First the young men were called into the army. Then the married men were pulled away from their beloved families and fields.

The day André Kovack left to be a soldier dawned

mockingly bright and clear. André leaned way out of the train window, smiling determinedly and waving. But the lump in his throat grew, seeming to choke him. Martha and the children waved back.

The train whistled mournfully. Martha shuddered and gripped little Anna's shoulder till the child cried out in pain. "I'm sorry, darling," Martha murmured, lessening her hold.

Slowly the train chugged out of the station. Anna burst out weeping. Young André, tears streaming unashamedly down his face, put his arm around his sister. Martha stood watching till she could see no more, then turned with leaden steps. "Come, children," she said simply.

At first the letters from André came regularly, and Martha answered faithfully. André wrote of his experiences in the army, trouble about the Sabbath, and his concern about the family. Martha told all the little happenings at home: what the children were doing, how the garden was progressing, how Batci the cow had birthed a new calf right out in the field.

Then came a pause in the letters that filled Martha with dread. Finally André's letter came, but the handwriting! Martha cried when she saw it. It was so shaky that she could hardly make out the words.

"My dearly beloved Martha," the letter began, "I have been terribly wounded, and unless the good

Lord sees fit to intervene, I have not long to live. I send my love to you and little André and Anna. Make sure they are raised in the truth—we must be an unbroken family in heaven."

Martha was distraught. And then came the news that her husband was dead. How the family survived the next few days, Martha never quite understood. Kind neighbors helped, and Martha leaned more heavily on God than ever.

Anxious to follow André's wish, she redoubled her efforts to teach her children the Bible. Every Sabbath they had a tiny Sabbath school and church service right in their own home.

But months later tragedy struck again. A terrible flu epidemic swept through the village. Martha nursed family and neighbors day after day. She was "a regular angel of mercy," as old Granny Haynal put it.

But one evening Martha took ill herself. As the fever raged, her strength drained. Days passed, and at last she realized she could not live. She drew André and Anna close and instructed them to love the Lord, study the Bible, and never forget the Sabbath.

"André dear," she said, "you are the oldest, so help your sister to read the Bible."

Shortly afterward Martha was laid to rest, awaiting the call of the Lifegiver. André and Anna were given a new home with their neighbor John Nagy and his wife.

The two children were heartbroken. "Oh, André, what will happen to us now?" sobbed Anna the next night.

"I don't know, sister, but our Jesus will take care of us," he comforted. "Here, I've brought our Bible. Let me read a little to you." Then they sobbed themselves to sleep.

Several days later farmer John came upon the children bent intently over their Bible. "Well, well," he boomed good-naturedly, "whatever are you reading?" But when he saw the book, anger suffused his usually pleasant face with an ugly red flush. He shook his pudgy fist. "The Bible? You're not to read that again, understand? I won't have heretics living in my house! Why, I'll beat you within an inch of your life if you ever read that book again!" Farmer John stalked off, breathing heavily from the exertion of waving his hands in the air and shouting.

From then on André and Anna had to be very careful when and where they read their Bible. Still, they were caught time after time. Each offense resulted in severe beatings.

Finally they fled to the woods to study the precious Bible. Even there farmer John found them, and punishment was swift and sure.

Finally the people of the village became aware of the situation. André Kovack's children were being mistreated! Indignation ran high, and soon John Nagy was brought to court.

When the circuit judge took his place that day, the courtroom was crowded. André was lifted onto a table so that he might be seen and heard.

"Is it true, André," the judge began kindly, "that farmer John Nagy beats you for reading the Bible to your sister?"

"Yes, sir," said André.

The examination continued. There was discussion, and then the judge said to André, "Now, since farmer John Nagy has beaten you so severely, you may decide his punishment."

"Oh, no, sir," came the clear voice of André. "The Bible says we should love our enemies. Turn him loose."

There was quite a stir in the courtroom. "What then should be done with the children?" someone asked.

André was consulted again. "Please, sir, we are willing to go back with Mr. Nagy."

The people in the courtroom were amazed. How could such kindness come from a child's lips?

Mr. Nagy's face had softened as no one could remember ever seeing it before. He wiped at his eyes furtively. Quite a few handkerchiefs could be seen in the crowded courtroom that day. André's attitude of Christlike forgiveness had made an impact.

"I will not punish the children again for reading the Bible," farmer Nagy promised. And so André and Anna went home with him.

The children were able to read their beloved Bible in the parlor now. At first farmer John listened occasionally from the privacy of the kitchen. His wife listened too. Then sometimes he would sit in the parlor with the children for a short while before he stalked out, half angry with himself for listening.

But the Holy Spirit was working on John, and more and more he found himself listening with eager, rapt attention. Eventually the day came when John concluded that he must study the Scriptures for himself and follow the Savior's invitation, "Come, John, follow Me."

John's conversion didn't happen in a blinding flash of light as with Saul in the Bible. Indeed, it took a long time. But one glad Sabbath morning the angels rejoiced as John Nagy stood before the little Adventist congregation in his tiny Hungarian village as its first Seventh-day Adventist pastor.

18

Touched by a Christmas Toad

by Christina Dotson

Stepping to the front of the room, I turned gracefully, closed my eyes, and began to sing. "Si-i-lent night, ho-o-ly night . . ."

"Bridget, look!" a voice whispered. "I can turn my eyelids inside out."

"All is calm . . ."

"Gross! Get away from me!"

"All is bright . . ."

"Mrs. Dunn, Mrs. Dunn! Make him stop!"

Unable to hold it in any longer, I burst out laughing—which, of course, put an end to my singing. Mrs. Dunn, our teacher, glared sternly at my schoolmates. Immediately the older kids stopped torturing the first graders and pasted on innocent smiles, trying to look like the perfect angels that half of them were dressed as.

We were in our church's otherwise empty sanctuary doing a final dress rehearsal of our Christmas program, now less than 24 hours away. The 13 other kids in my small church school barely filled up the front pew, yet their restless voices bounced off the walls as if the whole place were packed solid.

Mrs. Dunn sighed and dived into another lecture on proper sanctuary behavior. From my position alone up front, I yawned and scratched my ankle. I couldn't blame my friends for not paying attention while I practiced my solo for the zillionth time. It did seem rather pointless. Didn't Mrs. Dunn know I couldn't improve on perfection?

"You're like a great big roll of duct tape," my older brother, Tony, informed me later that afternoon as we piled into the vans to drive the three miles back to our school. "You're totally stuck on yourself."

"That is the dumbest thing I've ever heard," I replied.

Tony shrugged. "All I'm saying is that I don't think I'd go prancing around like a princess if I had a voice like a fork in a garbage disposal."

"If you pranced like a princess for any reason, I'd have you committed."

"Don't listen to him, Chrissy," my friend Ashley broke in. "You have a great singing voice."

I tossed my brother a triumphant smirk. "See? You're just jealous 'cause I'm the star of the program and all you get to sing is one lousy verse about Frankenstein."

"Frankincense," Tony growled. "You know I'm a wise man."

"Wise! That's a riot."

"What makes you the star, anyway? Just because you have the only solo—"

"I think you just answered your own question."

Tony leaned forward as Mrs. Dunn slid into the driver's seat. "Can I ride in the other van?" he asked. "I don't think there's room in here for me and my sister's ego."

The morning of the Christmas program dawned cold and bright. Not wanting to wrinkle my new dress, I sat uncharacteristically still in the backseat of the car as Mom drove us to church.

"You look like a peacock, the way you strut around," Tony proclaimed. "People are going to wonder what a peacock's doing at the stable in Bethlehem."

"They might wonder what a toad is doing there, too," I replied. "But I'm sure they'll recognize you."

"You know," said Tony, "I would think you'd be a little more concerned about spazzing out when you sing your solo."

I never should have listened to him, but I did. "Spazzing out?"

"Yeah, you know, panicking. Forgetting the tune.

Messing up the words. That happens sometimes, especially with overconfident people. They're so puffed up with pride that all of a sudden—poof—they spaz out!"

"Well, aren't you just full of the Christmas spirit," I snapped.

"At least I'm not full of Christmas conceit."

"Enough!" Mom called back at us. "This is no way for Christians to act. You're about to give a Christmas program!"

"Peacock," Tony muttered under his breath

"Ribbit," I croaked in reply.

Our pageant went just as we had practiced it a hundred times, complete with an angel choir that tripped over their robes and a Mary and Joseph who sat as far apart from each other as our stable scene would allow. As for me, I sat serenely in the front pew waiting for the program's end, when I would sing my solo. I was the grand finale.

When the time came, I got up and walked calmly to the front of the church. Now was my moment of glory.

I turned and faced the audience. Cameras flashed. Relatives beamed with pride. I stood up straight and tall, took a deep breath—and panicked! *Where did all these people come from? There must be millions of them! I didn't know our church fit so many people!*

In the middle of my nervous breakdown I suddenly

realized that the music had begun. I opened my mouth, but no words came out. I glanced over at the pianist. She stopped playing, frowned in confusion, and started up again. But now I wasn't sure if she was playing the introduction again, or if I should just start singing!

I was so panicked that by the time I got my voice to work, it came out piercingly high. "Sleep in heavenly pe-eace!" I was squeaking like an old barn door! A few people laughed. A lot more coughed, covering up laughs. I wanted to crawl behind the shepherds and hide. Instead, I finished the song as best I could and slunk back to my seat, humiliated.

For weeks I had dreamed of this day, of how perfectly I would sing and how everyone would congratulate me afterward. Yet when church was over, I stayed glued to the pew, determined not to budge until every last person had left.

It was Tony who came looking for me. I saw him coming and cringed. Now was his chance to gloat. "I thought you were supposed to sing a so-lo," he would probably say, "not a so-high." Or maybe he'd make some crack about how the song's title should be changed to "Silent Fright," since I'd been so terrified up there.

I sighed in defeat. No matter what he said, I knew I deserved it.

My brother plopped down next to me, and for a while he said nothing.

"Well, get on with it," I snapped. "Where's your 'I told you so'?"

"It really wasn't that bad," he said. "I hardly noticed the mistakes." My brother paused. "You do have a good voice."

My mouth fell open. "Is this some kind of joke?"

"What? Can't I be nice to my sister every once in a while?"

"But, but—" I sputtered. "But I acted like a total snob!"

"Yeah, well . . ." Tony shrugged. "It's Christmas."

The two of us fell silent for a long moment. Gradually my gaze traveled up to the stable scene at the front of the church. Suddenly, for the first time, I saw the scene for what it truly represented. It was all about Jesus, the Son of God, who was born in a smelly manger to teach us humility—a lesson I had just learned. It was about the One who later died to show mercy and kindness to a world that didn't deserve it . . . as my brother had just done for me.

"Thanks, Tony," I whispered with a smile. "And merry Christmas."

19

A Pirate Redeemed

by Melanie Scherencel Bockmann

Tobias closed his eyes and gripped the railing of the *Britannia*. The salty sea mist lightly sprayed his face as he imagined the adventure that lay ahead for him and the other missionaries on the island of St. Thomas.

He could almost see the red rooftops and shimmering Caribbean beaches that had been described to him. He wondered if the slaves they had been sent to teach would want to know God.

Suddenly shouts rang out. Tobias opened his eyes. What he saw instantly paralyzed him with fear. A smaller ship was coming up beside them at top speed, and Tobias knew that the images of death on the flag whipping in the wind meant only one thing: pirates!

"We're not going to surrender!" the captain of the

Britannia shouted as everyone gathered on deck. "We're going to fight!"

Tobias looked across the water and sucked in his breath. The pirates had pulled out their daggers and pistols. The huge black cannons that lined the side of the pirate ship were aimed directly at the *Britannia!*

Tobias grabbed the arm of one of the *Britannia's* deckhands. "We're no match for them!" he yelled above the noise. "We can't fight—they'll kill us!"

The deckhand jerked his arm away. "Trust me. You'd rather be dead than the prisoner of a pirate!"

Tobias ran to the cabin, where the other missionaries had gathered to fight—on their knees, praying to God.

Tobias knelt and began to pray. "God, there's nothing we can do to save ourselves. If You have really called us to bring hope to the slaves of St. Thomas, please save us from the pirates!"

When Tobias got back on deck, he saw that the pirate ship was even closer than before. Several of the pirates stood on the edge, getting ready to swing huge grappling hooks that would attach the ships together and make it easy for the pirates to take the *Britannia.*

"One, two, three!" Tobias heard the pirates shout as they swung their grappling hooks. But the moment they tried to swing the hooks, something strange happened. A violent wave came out of nowhere, jerking the pirate ship with such force that the men holding the ropes were thrown into the ocean!

Tobias could hardly believe his eyes. The captain of the pirate ship commanded a second line of men to throw grappling hooks. But just when they were ready to swing the ropes, they were also thrown into the ocean by a violent wave.

"Forget the grappling hooks!" Tobias heard the pirate captain shout angrily. "Fire the cannons!"

Tobias watched the pirates pull their cannons back into firing position and load the heavy iron balls. The cannons fired, but the cannonballs plopped harmlessly into the ocean.

Tobias's mouth dropped open. The ships were so close together that there was no way the cannons could have missed.

"Fire again!" Tobias heard the pirate captain shout.

Again and again the pirates fired their cannons, but all of the cannonballs plopped into the sea without ever touching their target. Tobias and the other missionaries began to cheer. God was stronger than the attackers, and He was answering their prayers!

The smoke from the firing cannons became so dense that it was impossible for the ships to see each other. The crew of the *Britannia* set their sails and began sailing away. When a sudden gust of wind blew away the dense smoke, Tobias and the other passengers could see that the *Britannia* had gained distance, and the pirates had given up the chase.

Tobias and the other missionaries arrived safely in St. Thomas and began their work of preaching the gospel. Five years later they gathered to celebrate and to thank God again for saving their lives.

During the celebration a stranger asked to come in. He was tall and strong, and he had a pleasant expression. Tobias thought he looked familiar.

"Are you the missionaries who were attacked by pirates on the *Britannia?*" he asked.

"Yes," Tobias answered. "Why do you ask?"

"Because," answered the stranger, "I was the captain of that pirate ship."

The missionaries gasped as the man continued. "I was amazed by what I saw that day. I asked around and was told how God answered your prayers. That made me want to know God, and I'm a different man now. I thought you might want to know the rest of the story."

Tobias realized that they had a lot more to celebrate. God not only saved them from a pirate, but He also saved a pirate from sin at the same time!

20

The Valentine Box

by Mary Chandler

I saw him sneaking through the long coat closet into our classroom during recess. His scraggly brown hair clung to his forehead, and his worn-out shoes squeaked.

As he shuffled into the room, he shot shifty-eyed glances all around to make sure no one was watching. I ducked behind the door. Scotty headed straight for the long table where 30 decorated valentine boxes awaited our Valentine's Day party the next day. I didn't say a word. I just waited to see what trouble Scotty was up to this time.

That kid was a real pest. When he wasn't smacking girls with snowballs and chasing us, he was picking fights with the boys. Scotty spent a lot of time in the principal's office—and he'd been at our school for only three weeks! I wished his dad would pack up the family and move back to where they came from. But like it or not, Scotty was here to stay.

The previous week our teacher, Mrs. Thompson, had asked each of us to bring a shoe box to class to decorate for a valentine box. We'd wrapped the boxes in white or red crepe paper and cut out paper hearts for the top and sides, adding doily lace to make the hearts look fancy. Candi and Brandi, the twins, glued red ribbons to their boxes, and Jay pasted some of those candy hearts that said "Be Mine" and other silly stuff on the top of his box. My best friend, Mary Helen, made a big heart out of red and white buttons for her box. Scotty didn't have a box, but Mrs. Thompson had brought extras. He gooped his valentine box up with hearts cut out of newspaper, which he colored bright-red, and pasted them so close together that you couldn't see where one started and the other one ended. It was a mess.

When we finished decorating our boxes, Mrs. Thompson had each of us print a name tag and paste it on the lid, right next to the slit where the valentines went. Peeking inside our box was off-limits— until Valentine's Day. Sometimes, though, when our teacher wasn't looking, we'd shake our box and try to guess how many valentines we had.

Most of the kids had already dropped valentines into the boxes, but not me. Instead of making my valentines this year, I was saving money to buy some valentines that had a little lollipop attached. I planned to get them right after school let out for the day. I needed my class list from my desk. That's when I spotted Scotty, up to no good, as always.

Scotty grabbed his bedraggled valentine box and shook it. Lifting the lids off several boxes on the table, he stole a valentine out of each one. When his greedy hands bulged with stolen valentines, he smiled and dropped them, one by one, into his box at the end of the table.

That greedy little thief! I thought. I almost jumped out from my hiding place to let him know I'd seen what he'd done. But Scotty was bigger than I was. I stayed put.

Scotty shoved his hands into his pockets, glanced around the room and out the window, and headed for the front door. When I heard those shoes squeaking down the hallway, I went into my classroom.

At the end of the table I saw the box—Scotty's box. I lifted the lid. Thirteen valentines addressed to someone else lay in that box, and that was all. Here it was, the day before Valentine's Day, and no one had given Scotty a valentine. No one.

I felt a big lump in my throat. I started thinking how awful it felt not to be included, like when Sondra got mad at me the previous week and didn't invite me to her birthday party. Or when Tom wouldn't let me play baseball just because I'm a girl and can hit more homers than he can.

After school I collected my money from babysitting my little brother and raided my piggy bank. I hurried over to the store and bought a packet of valentines. At home I got out my class list and wrote "Scotty" on every one of those valentines on the "To" line and added someone else's name, or "A Secret Admirer," or "Guess Who?" where the valentine said "From." Of course, I disguised my handwriting. Mama helped. Then we got out the colored paper, doilies, ribbons, and Mama's special sewing lace and did some homemade valentines for everyone else in my class, including Scotty, so he wouldn't get suspicious.

The next day my dad took me to school early. I went straight to Scotty's box and replaced the 13 stolen valentines with 30 fresh ones—complete with lollipops—plus 10 more homemade lacy valentines.

I can't describe the look on Scotty's freckled face when he opened his valentine box, or the smile that spread from ear to ear. You had to be there. I got another lump in my throat—the happy kind.

After that Scotty started being a whole lot nicer. Tom discovered that Scotty had a great pitching arm and asked him to be on his baseball team. Scotty stopped fighting and chasing the girls, too. Don't get me wrong—Scotty wasn't perfect, but who is? As for the valentines, I never told Scotty my secret. He didn't need to know.

21

The Perfect Dress

by Joan Beck

Is it ever hot in this gym!" Julie complained as she took a man's suit out of the donation box. "Where do men's suits go?" she asked Shannon.

"They go in those boxes on the table. We're going to leave them at Montemorelos University for the student ministers," Shannon said, pointing at the boxes. "I never thought we would get so many clothes donated to us for the church in Galeana." She wiped the sweat from her forehead.

The girls' Pathfinder club was preparing for a mission trip to Mexico. Julie and Shannon had assumed the task of packing donated girls' clothes in a box. As they worked, they judged the fashion chic of each garment they placed in the box.

"Oh, look," Shannon exclaimed as she held up "The Dress." It was a beautiful white designer dress, all sheer cotton and lace that seemed to say, "I am very expensive."

"Wow!" breathed Julie. The expressions on both girls' faces said that they had fallen in love with "The Dress." As each held it up to imagine how it would look on them, it was apparent that it would fit Julie.

Then they put "The Dress" aside. When all the boxes were packed and ready to go, everyone ate "reward" cookies and drank root beer floats. Julie and Shannon approached Mrs. Beck, the Pathfinder leader.

"Mrs. Beck, I found this dress in one of the boxes of donated clothes, and it would fit me perfectly. I just love it. May I have it? It was given to us to give away." Julie held the dress up to her body so Mrs. Beck could see how good it would look on her.

"Julie, you're right—that dress looks like it was made for you. But the dress was donated for the Mexican church members in Galeana, and it wouldn't be right to keep the clothes for ourselves. Sorry, sweetie. I'm sure there is a lovely young lady in Galeana waiting for this dress."

Julie sighed. "OK, I guess you're right."

Reluctantly Julie and Shannon returned to the girls' clothes box. They lovingly wrapped "The Dress" in tissue paper and placed it in its own box within the larger box.

During all the preparations for the mission trip

and the excitement of the actual trip, "The Dress" was forgotten. Everyone was totally involved in the sights, sounds, smells, and tastes of a new culture.

In Galeana the Pathfinders worked hard every day finishing Sabbath school rooms. They made house visits with Pastor Mannie and met all of his Mexican neighbors. They became very good at sign language when Pastor Mannie and Mr. Bill were not around to translate.

The clothes giveaway was to be Wednesday night before prayer meeting. Everyone bathed, ate quickly, and hurried back to the church to arrange the clothes on plastic stretched on the ground.

Then it was that "The Dress" reappeared. Julie and Shannon took the box that contained "The Dress" and placed it under the plastic, out of sight. Then they organized all of their clothes into piles and waited for the girls to arrive.

The Pathfinders had great fun helping the Galeana church members select clothes. Julie and Shannon, with their instinctive sense of fashion, were having the best time of all. One by one, they grabbed each girl, took her to their piles of clothes, and matched her with clothes that fit and looked lovely on her. After they had the girl all fashionably dressed, they would study her very carefully from all sides. Then, for some strange reason, they would look at each other, shake their heads "no," and send the girl on her way with her new wardrobe. "The Dress" remained hidden under the plastic.

As Pastor Mannie and Mrs. Beck watched the church members selecting clothes, a very poor elderly church member approached Pastor Mannie and had a long conversation with him in Spanish.

Pastor Mannie turned to Mrs. Beck. "Señora Morales has brought a neighbor family who are so poor that they don't have enough clothes for every-day wear. She would like to give up her portion of clothes and let this family have some clothes," Pastor Mannie explained.

Behind Señora Morales stood a very thin woman dressed in what looked like shreds of different clothes pieced together. She had two small boys dressed the same way. In fact, one wore nothing but a shirt. Peeking out from behind her skirt was a beautiful girl about 12 years old.

"Of course they can have clothes! And you tell Sister Morales that she is to select her portion of clothing also," Mrs. Beck responded.

All of the Pathfinders were told about the poor family and their need for clothes. James and Jeremy immediately took the little boys in hand and saw that they each had a stuffed toy to comfort them as they got fitted with their "new" clothes.

Brandy took the mother and started showing her all the women's clothes in her size. Julie and

Shannon eyed the girl, who still clung to her mother's skirt. They got Pastor Mannie to persuade the girl to come with them. What a wonderful time they had selecting clothes for her! She stood transfixed as one garment after another was brought out for her—even shoes and a coat.

Finally they decided the wardrobe was complete. Then they did their survey of her from all sides. After the first survey they started a second, while the girl stood clutching her clothes in her arms as if she was afraid they would take them back. They stopped in front of her, nodded their heads "yes," and hurried to the edge of the plastic, where they removed the box that contained "The Dress." They took "The Dress" out of the box and held it up to the girl. It was a perfect fit!

As the girl looked at the dress and realized that it was for her, tears began to run down her cheeks. She hugged Julie, Shannon, and Pastor Mannie; then she hugged them again.

Then she ran yelling to her mother with "The Dress" clasped to her heart. At that moment only Julie and Shannon were happier than that girl.

Monumental Accident

As told to Juliana Marin by Jorge Marin

I plunked away at the piano keys, staring vacantly out the window. School had been out only a week, and I was already bored.

All my friends were away on vacation, and the only thing there was to do was practice piano. And I was sick of that. My dad was convinced I was a musical genius, and he had me practicing several hours each day. OK, so I'd given several concerts, and for a 13-year-old guy I suppose that's something, but it got boring after a while.

I stretched and stood up. There was no way I was going to get anything done at the piano today. The sound of hammering lured me outside, which was where I'd much rather be. My dad was working on a 10-ton plaster sculpture in our backyard.

My father was a well-known sculptor. For years

he'd crafted various projects, but this was the work of his life. A public cemetery in our city of Medellín, Colombia, had asked for a 50-foot-high monument in bronze of the resurrected Christ. My dad and 15 crew members had been working on it steadily for months, and right now the entire structure was set up in our parking lot, staked to the ground with ropes and cables.

"Hey, Jorge," Luis called out as I walked outside. "Whatcha doin'?"

I sauntered over, looking up the ramparts to the statue's head. "Nothing to do," I answered. He grinned at me. I liked Luis. He was the youngest of the crew, and really friendly.

"When will the boss be back?" he asked.

I shrugged. "Sometime this afternoon. Errands."

I wandered around the formation with nothing much on my mind. Suddenly my gaze fell on our rickety old 1956 jeep, stationed forlornly near the garage. A plan started taking shape in my mind, one that I knew could get me in deep trouble if my dad found out. But then, he wasn't there! Suddenly the day didn't seem boring at all.

"Alberto," I called to the worker next to me, and then hesitated.

"I hear you, boy," he answered.

It was too late to back out. "Do you know how to drive?" I asked.

Alberto looked at me, startled. "Why, no, boy—I'm just a laboring man."

I began to smirk. "Would you like to learn?"

So that's how my driver training school started. I was taking time away from the workers, I was using the jeep without permission, and I was running the risk of getting everyone killed. But I knew how to drive, these guys were dying to learn, and Papa wasn't there. The lessons began.

Alberto was first. I explained everything in detail and then let him drive up from the gate, with me watching like a hawk and ready to grab the wheel if necessary. The other workers cheered as Alberto finally reached the parking lot and got out, white as a sheet but with a huge smile.

I kept everything under control, but since none of the guys had ever handled a vehicle before, the poor jeep jerked and turned off several times. When it became Luis's turn, however, he took to driving like a pro.

"Hey, where did you learn to drive, Luis?"

"No way, man. I've never driven before," he replied.

I settled back with a grin, knowing he was kidding. "Yeah, right, you drive better than I do. You've been holding out on us."

Luis laughed, but his steering didn't waver. We were nearing the parking lot. "OK, so what do I do now?"

"Ha, you tell me, pilot."

"No, I'm serious, Jorge. How do I stop?"

"Quit joking."

"Jorge! We're gonna crash! What do I do?"

With a yelp I realized that the whole thing was for real. "Brake! *Brake!*"

"This one?"

"No! That's the gas ped—*aaahh!*"

By the time I'd managed to take control, the jeep had zoomed halfway into the garage—taking the door with it.

The other workers rushed over and shoved the broken pieces of wood out of the way so that Luis and I could open our doors. I stepped out of the mess, unable to speak. The front of the jeep was all bent out of shape, the garage door was smashed, and we had missed by inches the main support cable of the 10-ton monument.

As we all stared, suddenly one of the workers snickered. In moments the whole crew was laughing hard enough to split, slapping Luis on the back and joking about what my dad would do when he found out. Someone said, "We won't let him find out," and they all set to work repairing the damage. The only ones not laughing were Luis and I.

"The boss is gonna be real angry with me for this, Jorge. I'm gonna get fired," he said.

The worst thing was that he was probably right. I

couldn't let him get in trouble for my sake, and I knew what I had to do.

"Luis, don't worry," I said as bravely as I could, although inside I was shaking. "It was my fault, and I'll be sure to tell that to my dad. I'll take care of it."

The workers were still laughing. I have no idea how they did it, but by the time the afternoon was over they'd totally fixed the garage door and had even hammered out the worst dents in the jeep. The remaining debris was picked up and swept away. In the twilight you'd never know.

The workers left, and I sat down on the porch to wait for my dad. I had no idea why he was taking so long. By the time he finally arrived, I had been sitting in the darkness for what seemed like eternity.

Papa was silent for a long time after hearing my tale. I kept waiting for the explosion, and I cringed when he finally spoke.

"Are your hands all right?"

I was so scared that I didn't even understand him. "What, sir?"

"I said, are your hands all right?"

I still didn't get it, but I showed him there was nothing wrong with them.

He grasped them strongly and said something I will never forget. "Your hands are your future, son. The jeep can be fixed with money, but your hands could not be repaired if they got ruined. You must use them to make beautiful music. They are more important." He sighed and let go of my hands. "Go. You have already punished yourself enough."

And that was it. He went inside, and I just sat there staring after him. No shouting, no whipping, just "the jeep can be fixed with money." What did he mean?

I walked outside and stared up at the monument. The Christ had His arms outstretched, palms up to gather His people. With a jolt I realized that His hands had been ruined on the cross, and the scars would always be there.

I stared back down at my own hands and suddenly felt sick at the thought of what could have happened. I guess my dad was right. What can be fixed with money is not that important. In his wise silence my father had taught me a lesson that punishment never could have.

I stuck my hands in my pockets and headed back toward the house. I still wasn't sure I'd turn into the great virtuoso my father wanted, since secretly I wanted to use my hands for sculpture instead of music. But at that moment I felt a burning desire to practice the piano.

23

Interrupted Christmas

by Wendy Hunt

I waited before opening my eyes on Christmas morning. Our playroom walls were covered with pictures of the perfect Christmas: snowy sleigh rides, relatives singing carols, children opening presents. I wanted this Christmas to be perfect.

Sorry—not happening. First, I lived on a tropical island, so no snow. Second, with few horses on the island, there would be no sleigh rides. And third, all my relatives lived miles away in the United States. Still, we did have a pile of presents in the living room. Christmas would be fun.

As I pulled on my jeans, my little brother popped into the room. His eyes sparkled. "Hurry, Wendy! Mom says we can open presents after breakfast!"

Christmas breakfast was special. I clattered down

the stairs and laughed when I saw Christmas-tree-shaped pancakes.

Dad had just prayed when the doorbell rang. I put down my fork. Dad looked at Mom. "Expecting someone?"

She shook her head and opened the door.

It was Tom, a young Chinese friend of my parents. He was holding a package wrapped in red. He bowed to Mom with an enormous smile. "Happy Christmas to you!" he said.

Mom couldn't help smiling back. "Merry Christmas, Tom. Er, can you come in?"

"But Mom! This is . . ." I started but stopped at a kick under the table. I shut my mouth and glared at my plate.

We moved to make room for Tom. Mom got him a plate. Tom ate lots of pancakes. It was his first time having pancakes, and he seemed to like them. I barely nibbled mine.

After breakfast the grown-ups sat and talked while we kids cleared the table. We didn't say much. We had only one thing on our minds—that pile of presents.

When we heard the front door close, we shot into the living room. Mom grinned at us. Dad rubbed his hands. "OK," he said. "Let's read the Christmas story from Luke 2." He settled himself in the rocking chair and opened the Bible. "In those days Caesar

Augustus . . ." He didn't get any further because the doorbell rang again. Dad put down his Bible and went to see who was there.

The Lieu family stood outside. Mr. and Mrs. Lieu were bowing and holding a red, wrapped present, and the little Lieus were bumping and pushing each other.

Dad stood there without saying anything. Mom ran a hand through her hair and stood up, putting on a welcoming smile. She turned to us.

"Scott, Wendy, why don't you show the kids the playroom? Maybe the Matchbox cars?" It wasn't really a question, and there wasn't really a choice. We shuffled to the playroom, followed by the Lieu children.

I don't remember much about those hours. The Lieus seemed to be everywhere, even though there were only four of them. The oldest was 5, and none of them spoke English. They had lots of energy. I didn't look at the pictures of perfect Christmases on the playroom walls.

Finally the Lieus left and our house stilled. We stood in the living room. Dad cleared his throat. "All right, let's go ahead with our Christmas reading." He opened the Bible again.

I stretched out on the couch (I deserved a break after the past two hours!) and closed my eyes, picturing the "No Vacancy" sign on the inn.

A loud knock interrupted Dad. He stopped reading. We froze. *Maybe*, I thought, *if we don't make noise, they won't know we're here and they'll go away!* The visitor knocked again.

Dad opened the door. It was Pastor Chien. He held out a present wrapped in red paper. He beamed at Dad. Dad invited him in. Mom welcomed Pastor Chien in Taiwanese. Then she led Scott and me to the kitchen.

"All right," she said. "The three of us can go to the market. I need a few things there anyway." She picked up her basket.

I frowned. "On Christmas? Is it even open? Doesn't it feel weird going shopping on Christmas?"

Mom stepped out the back door. "This isn't a holiday for Taiwanese. Their big festival is Chinese New Year next month. Today is mainly a . . ." She glanced toward the living room. "A day to visit friends."

"But when will we open presents?" Scott and I trailed behind Mom. Our feet dragged as we got farther away from those unopened presents.

"After lunch," said Mom.

It was 1:00 when we returned from shopping. Pastor Chien was disappearing down the road. Mom handed me the basket and unlocked the gate. I heard squawking and yelling from our yard. When the gate opened, we saw Dad and old Mrs. Yi running in circles. A squawking chicken darted past me. Another chicken, legs tied, struggled on the sidewalk.

Mom clapped a hand to her mouth, but not before a giggle escaped.

"Got you!" Dad dived on the chicken. He held it up like a trophy. Mrs. Yi hobbled over and tied its legs. She handed the upside-down chickens to Mom.

Dad got up. He was panting, and sweat dripped off his nose.

Mrs. Yi glowed at Mom. "I bring you Christmas gift," she said.

Mom held the struggling birds away from her body and made a bow to Mrs. Yi. "Shea-shea," she said. "Would you like to—er—come in for tea?"

It was mid-afternoon before Mrs. Yi took herself away. The freed chickens pecked happily in the backyard. We gathered in the living room, the unopened presents looming beside us.

Dad picked up the Bible and opened it to Luke 2. Then he looked at us. "You know, kids," he said, "it seems to me that we've got two reactions to Jesus' birth in this story."

I sighed and slumped. We'd had to wait all day, and now, when it was finally our chance to open presents, Dad was stalling.

"We've got the innkeeper, who had certain plans for his inn," continued Dad. "He wasn't willing, when Jesus needed a place, to give up his own ideas of what was important. And we've got the shepherds, who, when they heard about the new baby, dropped everything and hurried to Bethlehem."

He stopped, and I thought he might be done.

Instead, he cleared his throat. "Today we woke up with certain plans for our Christmas. But God had other plans. He had people for us to welcome. He had work for us on Christmas day. We thought Christmas was 'our day off,' but you know what? Christmas, more than other days, is a day to give up our wants and to give to others. With that in mind, go get a present you're giving to someone and hand it to them."

It was fun opening our presents that evening, but the funny thing is that I don't even remember what I got that Christmas. What I do remember are the people God brought to our door that Christmas, the people He gave us to love. Jesus was born so He could die. And when I die to my own plans, I truly receive God's gift.